Standing on Mountains

Rediscovering & Reclaiming Neglected Guiding Bible Truths

For the Christianson Family
Chad, Ansley, Caden, Chance & Cannon

Table of Contents

1. *An Amusing and Timely Story*

The *Bible** relates a funny account of a riot started in a town near the western shores of modern-day Turkey (*hereafter, *"God's Word"* will generally be used, instead of *"Bible,"* as a fairer representation of the Book's true Source and ultimate Author − it would be wise if publishers would follow this practice to cause less confusion about its contents and, therefore, its importance):

> There arose a great disturbance about the Way [a First Century expression for Christianity] . . . they were furious and began shouting: "Great is Artemis of the Ephesians!" Soon the whole city was in an uproar . . . The assembly was in confusion: Some were shouting one thing, some another. ***Most of the people*** <u>did not even know why they were there</u>. ^{Acts 19: 23-32}

Timely and Instructive How?

If you polled a large number of people going into various buildings today, asking them why they were there, most would give a good answer *except* those going into churches – these folks would, more often than not, studder and stammer until finally coming up with some ill-conceived cliché. And many of them would have been going to church, week after week, for years! Yet most would "not [meaningfully] even know why they were there." Not so unlike feeling they *have to* or *should* visit a relative out of a sense of obligation, some people still go to church and try to read *God's Word* while many others have finally stopped. It seems now like even many church leaders seemingly do not know why they are there.

In the words of a wise woman of yesteryear we might legitimately raise the same question she asked:

https://www.youtube.com/watch?v=U80ebi4AKgs

Three times she asked the pertinent question only to come to the same conclusion many come to today about church – "I don't think there is anybody back there."

Distractions, Distractions and Yet More Distractions

We know that, in one generation, the Christian Church has moved (as a general and most typical rule) from far less "there" time, in many churches previously meeting and teaching four times a week to now generally once: from Sunday School and Sunday morning, Sunday and Wednesday evening services to meeting a single time on Sunday morning (or Saturday evening). And in the past, the primary reason they were there was much more obvious, focusing on instruction in *God's Word*.

While distractions have always been an issue, keeping people from focusing on what is most important while majoring on relative molehills, they have increased dramatically in recent years. These diversions tend to make our spiritual "eyes" bad – blind to, confused about or out of focus to God's great (what we here refer to as) "Mountain" truths.

Historical Distractions – Two somewhat related digressions from the vital truths and teachings of Christ are the pride issues of:

- Focusing on other people's sins – sins of others (especially the current "hot button" sin issues of society in general) have always been favorite preaching and teaching topics; they are safe because they don't tread on too many toes of "faithful" church attenders.
- Denominational distinctives – beyond the issues of differences in what are considered sin, churches have varying interpretations and emphases of doctrines and extra-*Biblical* traditions. These, again, are generally safe preaching topics.

Seeing ourselves in others' sins can be a helpful teaching tool and there is nothing wrong with distinctives that are matters of taste and acknowledged as such. But when either (or both) become time-consuming emphases and matters of pride, they blind us to seeing God's greater truths.

Increasing Modern Distractions

And within a single generation the American church has been busy formulating new and novel church credos:

- Politics and Elections – the common current perception of those both inside and outside the church is that all-too-often churches closely mirror Washington and our State Houses at their worst: highly politicized with the result of being harsh, divisive, self-righteous, looking out for "our rights" . . . aligning with, supporting and becoming seeming Democrat or Republican mouthpieces and shills.

- Motivational, psychological, self-help . . . typically the teachings of more conservative, up by the boot-strap, churches focusing on temporal (versus eternal) topics.
- Social justice issues – paralleling today's "Progressive" agendas approving, even championing, causes that a few short years ago were generally believed wrong and unacceptable.
- "Worship" – many churches (especially those with younger attendees) have pivoted away from a focus and time devoted to preaching and teaching to a much greater stress on "worship" (singing).

In contrast, knowing *God's Word*, anchored by His Mountain truths, is the way to make our spiritual eyes better and better, to place the molehills of life in proper perspective in relation to far more important temporal and eternal realities and truths affecting all aspects of life: physical, emotional, spiritual . . .. *God's Word*, ingested on a regular basis, accomplishes this task and is **the key** Grace provided to keep our spiritual "eyes" healthy and focused.

People in any field are victorious only if they minimize the unnecessary distractions from their key goals. Thus, what we consider central vs. distractive (Mountain vs. molehill) will ultimately best define our success in any endeavor, including our spiritual/eternal development. And even the best church is not capable of spoon-feeding an adequate diet of *God's Word* so that we, personally, must regularly "be in" His Word to filter life's many mole-hill distractions.

Maybe the greatest responsibility of the church is helping its members maintain proper perspective and focus on Christ and eternity. As such, they should be warning against these diversions, not leading their members further into them corporately and personally.

Sadly, however, the church is now more and more splintered with the concern being not only "Where's the beef," but even more basic: "What is the beef? Why are we *really* here?

God & His Word Cancelled?

The very natural consequence of the all-too-common distractions away from *God's Word* is that His Word is being correspondingly "cancelled" by those with non-Biblical agendas or a focus on minor issue seemingly treated as major life and death concerns that they are not. Many churches have failed to heed one of Jesus' great warning and, as a result, replaced their preserving Gospel "salt" with sugar and dimmed or extinguished their light to appease the surrounding decaying and darkening society. Mt 5:13-16

One institution after another has been muzzled in the face of this cultural tsunami to political correctness. Media, education, government (international and domestic), businesses and finally the church probably to the greatest degree. These recently developed, in church, distractions are probably the eggs laid by the chickens seemingly fearing man far more than God. Yet, even in

process of everyone trying to "be nice" and get along, those giving in to the PC pressures
are not commended, but berated and lectured even more harshly!

As just one example, who today would dare to publicly question the credibility and
reasonableness of the LGBTTQQIAAP (and whatever other letters have been added more
recently) lobby? If they did, they would be quickly and roundly shamed and cancelled to the
fullest extent of today's power brokers' influence and abilities.

In this environment, then, it should be no surprise that *God's Word* has been largely cancelled,
dismissed as regressive and divisive by church critics while, at the same time, being increasingly
ignored **in church** in a silent rejection of its importance and validity. Why waste time, then, to
read it personally if the church has seemingly abandoned and cancelled it?

But the simple fact is that if we (personally or corporately) cancel *God's Word* we effectively
correspondingly cancel God in our lives. For **only** in and through His Word do we find what
God has to say to us, it being **the** means through which He trains us to hear His Voice and to
distinguish between His Voice and the many other, often much louder, competing voices we
hear all around us. *God's Word* is His ***only*** written Word given us. So, if *God's Word* falls on deaf
ears and unresponsive hearts, we have effectually cancelled Him in our lives!

Happily, though, there are still large numbers of people who have not cancelled God and His
Word and their testimony is that He still speaks and, in contrast to the increasingly louder more
radical opposing voices, He speaks in His Word more clearly than ever. Canceling by many has

counter-intuitively become a great blessing to those who have been awakened like Jesus' historic disciples to His questioning if they intended on leaving (canceling) Him as so many others were:

> "Lord, to whom shall we go? **You have the words of eternal life**. We have come to believe and to know that you are the Holy One of God." Jn 6:66-69

God and the cancelling of His Word is (as it always has been) a largely personal matter. Little has really changed. For *God's Word* warns us literally thousands of times and in many ways as one of its top themes that we must always **personally** (churches are not saved, individuals are!) remain vigilant and CAREFUL to keep *God's Word* real and active in our lives. There are so many great Mountain verses about this danger (because it is such an important and common stumbling block issue) we can here only highlight a few examples:

> "If you do what is right, will you not be accepted? But if you do not do what is right, **sin is crouching at your door**; it desires to have you, but you must master it." Ge 4:7

> "There will be false teachers among you." 2Pe 2:1

> We must pay more careful attention, therefore, to what we have heard, so that we do not drift away. Heb 2:1

God's Word would be a *much* shorter book (maybe pamphlet size) if He were to simply state His "to dos" so we could follow these teachings. But instead, He has to warn us in great detail about many sins that are "crouching at our doors" that can potentially lead us astray and ultimately

7

eternally destroy us. The following, if the many warnings were not necessary, would be much of what God needed to tell us:

> Jesus says, "'Love the Lord your God with all your heart and with all your soul and with all your mind. This is the first and greatest commandment. And the second is like it: 'Love your neighbor as yourself.' **All** the Law and the Prophets hang on these two commandments." Mt 22:37-40
>
> "So in everything, do to others what you would have them do to you, for **this sums up** the Law and the Prophets." Mt 7:12

Looking at just one example of God's "be careful" warnings, He provides very short, simple and unmistakably clear guidance, *for our good,* on the issue of sexuality. Yet in His Word, He details, in many pages and examples, warnings of the almost countless sexual sins and perversions men routinely and repeatedly engage in to their harm. Thus, God's warnings are critical so we don't find ourselves taking one step forward in faith only to be cursed by 2 or many steps back as we are deceived by the increasingly "legal" (to man, not God!) sin voices crouching at our doors waiting to capture, master and ultimately destroy us – to cancel God and His Word in our lives.

There are two *New Testament* books with these warnings as their main theme (with all books of *God's Word* touching on the BE CAREFUL! theme to one degree or another):

> "Dear friends, although I was very eager to write to you about the salvation we share, I felt I

had to write and urge you to contend for the faith that was once for all entrusted to the saints. For certain men whose condemnation was written about long ago have secretly slipped in among you. They are godless men, who change the grace of our God into a license for immorality . . ." Jude 1:3-4

"I am astonished that you are so quickly deserting the one who called you by the grace of Christ and are turning to a different gospel – which is really no gospel at all. Evidently some people are throwing you into confusion and are trying to pervert the gospel of Christ." Gal 1:6-7

And any thought that *God's Word* is obsolete, as so many (even in today's churches) think and teach, is not God's viewpoint – for to God, His Word is timeless and, at most, a few days old:

"Do not forget this one thing, dear friends: With the Lord a day is like a thousand years, and a thousand years are like a day." 2Pe 3:8

Knowing we must ALWAYS BE CAREFUL is one key reason we must know God's Mountain verses.

Much More Could be Said . . .
. . . and initially was, but was deleted so as not to be a further distraction from our goal and purpose – highlighting key Mountain verses and passages in *God's Word*. So, let's get right to Standing on Mountains – rediscovering and reclaiming neglected key guiding *Bible* truths after a short overview and introduction to Mountain Climbing – Summary and Caveat.

2. Mountain Climbing – Summary and Caveat

In as few pages as we have here it is obvious this is not going to be comprehensive *Bible* teaching, but we can hope, after highlighting and contemplating these key verses, for a much greater understanding of the *Bible's* important foundational themes. These Mountain verses provide us improved perspective (from God's point of view) to keep us from being distracted and potentially, in the process, missing His Way.

The following are key Mountain verses and passages EVERY authentic Christian should readily know . . . they are essential to understanding the rest of *God's Word*. We are NOT saying knowing these verses provides an immediately full and clear picture of <u>all</u> that *God's Word* says – nobody has achieved this level of insight no matter how smart they are or however diligently they have studied *God's Word*. Rather what we are attempting in this short overview is to highlight, draw into the immediate conscious, the key Mountain verses and truths as a foundation and framework to better grasp *God's Word* through its key themes.

Also, these are not 25 or so isolated thoughts and truths, they are linked synergistically – they provide better understanding of other verses and passages in *God's Word*. As we read more and longer, they will form a "tapestry" providing support for each other – a more cohesive picture will emerge and become clearer and more distinct as we proceed in reading *God's Word*.

So, here are the Mountain verses we are highlighting – let's go through them to see how many of the blanks you are already able to complete:

✓ Jesus warned, "You have a fine way of rejecting the commandment of God in order to establish your _____!"

✓ *God's Word*'s defined "goal of your faith is _____."

✓ The very first recorded public spoken word of Jesus ("_____") and a short explanation of what it means.

✓ "The law was given through Moses; _____ came through Jesus Christ."

✓ What is "Grace"? Other than "The unmerited favor of God," the most typical (weak) definition given us.

✓ God "gives grace to _____."

✓ "God chose _____."

✓ Where, in *God's Word*, is His best and most complete "picture" of eternal salvation?

✓ We are Saved BY "_____."

✓ We are saved FOR: "to do _____."

✓ "The work of God is to _____."

✓ "The Word of God is _____."

11

✓ "And now, Israel [today – Christian] what does the Lord your God ask of you but to fear the Lord your God, to walk in obedience to him, to love him, to serve the Lord your God with all your heart and with all your soul, and to observe the Lord's commands and decrees that I am giving you today _____?"

✓ Jesus says: "If you love me, you will _____."

✓ "_____, if you hear his voice, _____."

✓ "I have spoken to you of _____ and you do not believe; how then will you believe if I speak of heavenly things?"

✓ "_____ and all these things will be given to you as well." What does this *really* mean – what is Jesus' promise here?

✓ "In the beginning God _____." "This is easy!" most people will say. But have we really been taught or considered anything beyond its superficial implications?

✓ "_____whoever blasphemes against the Holy Spirit will never be forgiven; he is guilty of an eternal sin." How and why is this maybe the most encouraging verse in *God's Word*?

✓ Jesus says: "_____ you can do nothing."

✓ "I can do everything through _____."
✓ Do you know how to make the devil flee from you? _____ & _____.
✓ "There remains, then, a _____ for the people of God."
✓ "Whoever lives by the truth comes into the light, so that _____."
✓ "Examine yourselves to see _____."

  In the following chapters, we will fill in the blanks for each of these key *God's Word* points and verses to identify how and why they are thematic, not just random, verses – how they are great Mountain verses in *God's Word*, truths we need to keep in our conscious, not subconscious, minds. These are key "slotting" truths to make sense of what we read in or are taught about *God's Word* as well as helping us identify and reject errors and distractions when confronted with them, and we will encounter them (sometimes even in church).

Suggestions About Reading *God's Word* & this Short Book

  Start and read through the *New Testament*. Read normally, **don't** let what you don't grasp at first sidetrack you because God may in the next sentence, paragraph or chapter make your question(s) clear OR it may be a while before an answer comes. I am still waiting to understand some things and I fully expect to have open questions when I die.

  Sadly, we live in an age of too frequent passivity, expecting or hiring others to do what we don't want, or feel inadequate, to do. The practical difference between an attitude of passivity versus active seeking of Better? "How much do I **have** to do?" vs. "How much **can and should** I do based on considering the relative importance of a life area or issue?" *God's Word* is of critical importance to any authentic Christian – to anyone truly interested in knowing God Better. As such, we cannot "hire" this out to our pastor to do for us.

For those who have, in the past, tried and failed to read and understand *God's Word*, we must understand **no one** has the desire to read *God's Word* without God's Grace nor will we understand what we read without His Grace. Thus, our prayer and hope for understanding what we read in *God's Word*? That of the Psalmist:

Open my eyes that I may see wonderful things in your law. ^{Ps 119:18}

For there are certainly many many wonderful things in *God's Word*, promises and blessings just waiting for us to seek and find them.

And in reading this short book, we suggest you not "speed" read it, but reflect on and contemplate each Mountain verse or passage being highlighted, maybe even taking a day or two between each chapter.

So now, let's look, as our first Mountain verse, to a key warning of Jesus that will clear out a lot of the religious undergrowth and debris entangling and keeping us from scaling these great Mountain promises and blessings.

Even though not referring to *God's Word* when he said it, William Blake's quote is nowhere more applicable than when we "meet" God's great Mountain truths in His Word:

Great things are done when men and mountains meet.

3. *Jesus warns, "You have a fine way of rejecting the commandment of God in order to
_____!"*

"You have a fine way of rejecting the commandment of God in order to **observe your own traditions!**" Mk 7:9

Ouch! And this from Jesus Himself. We too often make molehills out of mountains and mountains out of molehills, keeping us from understanding what is key, what is not, why we are seeking God and how He says we are to do this.

The vast majority of people already have some ideas and opinions about Christianity, the *Bible*, churches, preachers, hypocrites . . . in the church. And some with the least first-hand experience and knowledge have the strongest opinions. Most people who have in the past attended (or are currently attending) church have been "indoctrinated" to one degree or another with certain denominational doctrines and distinctives supported by preaching, teachings, books and literature effectively placed on par with, or even above, *God's Word* (judging by the amount of time and emphasis placed on them as compared to *God's Word*).

Add to this that much has been written and taught in well-intended efforts to explain *God's Word* that, in the end, only complicate and obscure His truths. There are *Bible* experts who certainly need to probe, research, write and discuss among themselves theories to keep us laymen on the right path (just as there are experts in every field working beyond any limits mere users of their products, services, etc. need go). But the average laymen had better tread very carefully into these probings, writings and discussions. And these authorities in religion (or supposed professionals in *God's Word*), need to likewise take care they do not distract and confuse simple users and, in the process, do more harm than good. All to say, if we stay focused on what *God's Word* says (not what others by "deep" thought and extension say it *really* means) we can, at a user level, understand it. And a great theme of *God's Word* confirming this is that understanding the truths of *God's Word* is possible with (and only by) God enlightening its readers through His indwelling Holy Spirit that all authentic Christians possess. The Holy Spirit is THE KEY to understanding *God's Word*.

Much like the Bereans (commended in *Acts 17* as those who "received the message with great eagerness and examined the Scriptures every day to see if what Paul said was true"), we must be well-schooled in and by *God's Word* to properly mitigate the many distractions of the world and even within the church itself. All this goes a long way toward explaining how many, early 20th Century and prior, poorly educated humble farmers understood *God's Word* far better than most of us today with all our other books, podcasts, videos . . . they **only** (a very BIG only!) had *God's Word* and the Holy Spirit's leading into what it meant to them personally.

Reading *God's Word* objectively for what it clearly tells us (unfettered by our preconceived biases, traditions and other ingrained distractions) is not so unlike the puzzle pictures we have seen of what we have been told ahead of time is a vase only to find later it is really two faces:

If we have been told and taught one interpretation and meaning of, say, a *Bible* verse it is often very difficult to "undo" this impression even when a better meaning is given. Or if the *Word of God* is mixed with man's invented and highly developed (over the years – often centuries) traditions it is likewise hard to separate truth from error. With these very common realities in mind, Jesus warned as one example (as He continues to warn us in many ways today):

> The Pharisees and scribes questioned Jesus: "Why do your disciples not walk according to the tradition of the elders? Instead, they eat with defiled hands."
> Jesus answered them . . .
> "You have disregarded the commandment of God to keep the tradition of men."
> He went on to say, "You neatly set aside the command of God to maintain your own tradition . . . Thus you nullify the word of God by the tradition you have handed down. And you do so in many such matters." Mk 7:5-13

In another case, early in the *New Testament* (beginning in *Matthew 5*) we find Jesus' warning against several very common, but false, teachings – He refocuses His listeners (just as he does His listeners who read His Word today) by telling them again and again:

"You have heard that it was said . . . But I say to you . . ."

And this instruction and warning was to the *most* religious of His time – the ones who ultimately had Him killed because they sincerely, but wrongly, thought their traditions and distorted interpretations were right and above the clear teachings in *God's Word*. And the exact same errors are happening today as we so often read and interpret, without questioning, through the lens of "You have heard that it was said . . ." denominational distinctives and traditions.

If we are really going to read and understand *God's Word* we must follow its direction to:

Test ***everything*** that is said. Hold on to what is good. 1Th 5:21

We must seek to be like the Berean Jews, mentioned above, who were declared to be "of more noble character than those in Thessalonica, for they received the message with great eagerness and examined the Scriptures <u>every day</u> to see if what Paul said was true." Acts 17:11

Similarly, we are warned:

See to it that no one takes you captive through philosophy and empty deception, **according to the tradition of men**, according to the elementary principles of the world, rather than according to Christ. Col 2:8 and

"Do not go beyond what is written." ^{1Co 4:6}

Simply knowing this great Mountain warning in *God's Word* to "Test everything that is said. Hold on to what is good" will help tremendously in overcoming the challenges and potential traps of misleading traditions.

Traditions are not necessarily wrong and bad, but **all** traditions need to be considered in light of and "under" *God's Word's* teachings (not as on par with it) in much the same way that minor truths in *God's Word* can be wrongly elevated to mountain status and become harmful teachings, traditions and practices if we are not careful.

Who does not want, at their time of eternal judgement, to hear Jesus commend them with: "You had a fine way of listening to me and what I told you, testing and rejecting the traditions of men contrary to what I told you in my Word. You sought, valued and observed my teachings – great job!" so as to successfully accomplish the goal of their faith?

But wait a minute – what exactly is the goal of our faith? Do we know? Have we been told? Yes, *God's Word* tells us but sadly few have been taught this great truth. Let's correct this shortcoming by looking at it as our next Mountain verse.

4. *"The goal of your faith is* _____*."*

We began our discussion of Mountain verses looking at a humorous story of a riot in an ancient city, with *God's Word* remarkably noting that "Most of the people did not even know why they were there." We analogized this to the current reality that if we asked people why they were going to church, most would have a hard time providing a good answer. Likewise, if we made the question even more pointed and personal by asking: "What is the goal of **your** faith?" we would most often encounter a "Huh?" or simple dazed look.

How and why is this the case when *God's Word* clearly tells us? If we are not told and taught this soon after we are born again, we seriously risk:

- Heading off in a wrong direction or
- Being discouraged, distracted and possibly giving up – running down one rabbit trail or dead-end after another (this was my experience and I don't think I am unique in this respect).

At a minimum, much time and progress are lost.

Goals are hopes defined and crystallized and hope is a great motivator. We need God's single given goal to keep us spiritually focused and encouraged because:

- In "good" times we incline towards getting caught up in, being distracted by and living for all the fun we can supposedly have, only to find ourselves, at some point, away from

God, entangled and in bondage to one sin or other.
• In times of trials we are apt to devote all our thoughts, efforts, energy and emotions to "just getting back to normal" without remaining focused on the great goal of our faith and understanding these trials can aid us in achieving this end or
• When routine is the norm we have a tendency to become bored and less than focused on what is by and far most important in life, accomplishing the salvation of our eternal souls.

A good goal is important to keep us properly focused in all seasons. And what could be more practical, important and motivating than God's provided answer to the great goal in our most critical life and death issue?

"The goal of your faith, **the salvation of your souls**." 1Pe 1:9

That the guiding goal of our faith is the salvation of our soul is a truth we must return to and replay over and over and over to test what we are doing and why. This certainly is a vital Mountain truth that should always be uppermost in our minds!

In an imaginary poll asking people for the goal of their faith, even if we gave them time to provide thoughtful answers, most replies would cluster around a theme of what **we must do for God** to please Him – something along those lines.

Let's be honest, serious Christian faith is appealing to very few people because it is caricatured (and so often presented by Christians themselves) as sacrificing much now with a promise of more later, after we die. Add to this that (caricature or reality) the more religious people are so often seemingly the most self-righteous, intolerant and least happy people.

   In any case, a goal wrongly focused in majoring on what we must do for God (as we will look at a little later) is not a great motivator, rather it is something to dread. No wonder, with this prejudiced notion (as discussed in the previous chapter showing how we can incorrectly see a vase as two faces or vice versa by preconceived biases), that the God-given defined goal of our faith is seldom known and highlighted. And sadly, this error is commonly the same for pastor and preacher as for laymen in the pews. The Mountain truths?

> The goal of your faith, the salvation of your souls.[1Pe 1:9]

> I press on toward the goal to win the prize for which God has called me heavenward in Christ Jesus. [Phil 3:14]

God, in His Word, could not make it clearer or simpler – the goal of our faith is the salvation of our souls. Having this goal firmly implanted in our hearts and minds is a very real motivation to "stay the course" in times of trials and when life seemingly becomes routine, and thus tends toward boredom and resulting sin. It helps keep us focused on eternity and its promised prize:

> . . . a faith and knowledge resting on the hope of eternal life. [Titus 1:2]

> How shall we escape if we ignore such a great salvation? [Heb 2:3]

23

Can you "feel my pain" (frustration, shock . . .) at going years before "seeing" these two initial great Mountain truths (having poor spiritual eyes – being distracted by molehills), until I *finally* began to see and understand these great foundational truths? I don't know how much time was lost, but it was unnecessary because these guiding Mountain truths were (and for those being born again today are) not being simply and clearly taught early! This is wrong.

"You have a fine way of rejecting the commandment of God in order to observe your own traditions!" Mk 7:9

The goal of your faith, the salvation of your souls. 1Pe 1:9

And, likewise, our third great Mountain verse example that follows is maybe the most important one-word quote of all times, yet sadly, again, it is not emphasized today in the vast majority of churches.

5. *The Very First Recorded Public Spoken Word of Jesus and a Short Explanation of What it Means (versus its often man-defined traditional gutted and distorted application).*

We have looked at a Mountain warning about the very common way in which we, especially church-going folks, so often reject *God's Word* in favor of our traditions as well as the clarifying and focusing Mountain goal of our faith, the salvation of our souls. Nowhere are these Mountain verses more important than in looking at Jesus' first recorded public Word found very early in the *New Testament's Matthew 4*.

Just as knowing our goal (the salvation of our souls) is vital to keep us focused, being told Jesus' mission is necessary to piece together what He tells us in *God's Word*, both what He says and what others say about Him. And this is revealed to us. For immediately prior to His first recorded public Word we are told "From that time on Jesus began to preach . . .," further highlighting this was not a random or minor thought – this was His preaching theme from the very beginning of His public ministry continuing through today.

And sadly, we immediately see how our traditions, in minimizing what He is here saying, have clouded and confused our understanding while, at the same time, failed to firmly tie together His and our joint goal, the salvation of our souls.

> From that time on Jesus began to preach, "**Repent**, for the kingdom of heaven has come near." Mt 4:17

"I know and have repented!" many people will confidently proclaim – "I can even remember the time and place I did it. I have repented and am saved." But a fair and open-minded further reading in *God's Word* makes it totally clear an initial, one-time, repentance is just the beginning of an authentic Christian life. The initial repentance **will and must be** followed by more and on-going repentances, a developing discipline of repentance.

Yet "Repent," as a vital Christian discipline, is not taught in many churches while others often lead us to believe it is "Wham Bam thank you Ma'am," all done (the salvation of our souls fully accomplished) in an instant with a single repentance. If this were true *God's Word* would be a lot of wasted words and paper! The frequent tradition of man in the treatment of this first recorded Word, first command, of Jesus is a parody of its truth.

From the summit of this one-word Mountain command (not an overstatement to say the most important quote of all times), we can view and begin to take in the whole of our salvation – "Repent" is a very very high Mountain command! For <u>all</u> change is accomplished only through repentance. Thus, repentance is the single thread tying together the unbreakable tapestry of salvation from beginning to end, from being born again through our God-given sanctification to glorification at death and entry to heaven.

And what the error of tradition has so often failed to highlight is that, by definition, "Repent" is always and necessarily two-sided: From → To, not just a simple "acceptance" and belief in Jesus, rather it is a rejection of what we formerly believed and lived to a new, opposite, belief and life (just the thing religionists too often do not want and will not do – they will add a nominal belief in Jesus to their life, but not to any degree that requires substantial change).

The "Repent" Jesus is commanding here (as made obvious in His later teachings) is not the "invite Jesus into your life," the part-time and limited to certain aspects of life proclamation of many professing Christians, but a repenting towards the Master/servant (*God's Word*) paradigm of a newly developing 24/7/365 life – ALL areas and hours of life, beginning at a point to be continued throughout life until our earthly deaths, time here ends and we pass over into eternity.

"Repent," the clearly most important and practical quote of all times, is a Mountain imperative that, by the leading, teaching and reminding of the Holy Spirit, will become the foundation of the daily changes, in all areas of life, required to improve and progress – to be increasingly sanctified. Seeking repentance (versus our previous dread and rejection of correction) will be our new nature. Jesus' simple one-word life lesson reminds us daily of His great wisdom compared to the foolishness of the world that confirms even the worst in others rather than inspire them to repent (to change to Better).

Count the Cost!

Unlike the weak, wrong and useless message so often "peddled" by professing Christians to "Just believe . . .," Jesus proclaims the impossible (without His continuing Grace from new birth until death) repentances that accompany salvation. A remarkable paradox and great on-going challenge of Christian faith? It is not that life becomes harder and harder, rather life becomes increasingly impossible apart from Christ, thus requiring on-going growth "in the grace and knowledge of our Lord and Savior Jesus Christ" [2Pe 3:18] as He calls us to repent, repent, repent:

> Large crowds were traveling with Jesus, and turning to them he said: "If anyone comes to me and does not hate father and mother, wife and children, brothers and sisters – yes, even their own life – such a person cannot be my disciple. And whoever does not carry their cross and follow me cannot be my disciple.
>
> "Suppose one of you wants to build a tower. Won't you first sit down and estimate the cost to see if you have enough money to complete it? For if you lay the foundation and are not able to finish it, everyone who sees it will ridicule you, saying, 'This person began to build and wasn't able to finish.'
>
> "Or suppose a king is about to go to war against another king. Won't he first sit down and consider whether he is able with ten thousand men to oppose the one coming against him with twenty thousand? If he is not able, he will send a delegation while the other is still a long way off and will ask for terms of peace. In the same way, **those of you who do not give up everything you have cannot be my disciples**." [Lk 14:25-33]

In other words, we don't back into Repent, we must consciously and thoughtfully decide what we are going to do and set aside (by Grace – we can't do it without Grace) everything that would potentially impede it. Tradition does not teach this; it is simply too hard (which is true) unless we Repent as Jesus intended and are truly born again: indwelled and empowered by His Holy Spirit.

Looking at "Repent" from another viewpoint, very few things "stick" with people because they fail to understand what Repent really entails, not trying to fit something more into an existing, already busy, life, but "tearing life down," building it from the bottom (foundation) up, differentiating between the "if <u>I</u> have time . . .," "if <u>I</u> can . . .," focusing instead on what God can do through us under this new, streamlined and focused, paradigm! Ad hoc living produces ad hoc results — only a life built in a thoughtful, well-planned and executed manner (similar to a physical structure) is going to result in a good outcome. Yes, "Repent" means so much more than commonly taught in church.

So let's next briefly look at what we can expect from Jesus, what he promises His followers, His "repenters." – no, not new cars, health and wealth . . . as some teach, but much better . . .

6. *"The law was given through Moses;* _____ *came through Jesus Christ."*

   Once told, it is obvious that the goal of our faith is the salvation of our souls, a sure Mountain truth. Likewise, it should be obvious that we must Repent to this goal again and again (not be sidetracked by distracting traditions) if we hope to accomplish it.

   This being true, we might logically ask: "What has Jesus offered in the way of helping us achieve our all-important goal?" There is no use thinking and seeking X if God, in His Word, clearly tells us He offers Y. And He does tell us, but for whatever reason this great Mountain truth is not early, routinely or consistently taught so that many people **are** seeking X, not Y. This leaves us to return to the great Mountain verse (Jesus warned, "You have a fine way of rejecting the commandment of God in order to establish your traditions!") as the likely answer as to why we are not told this vital promise.

   Few people will be surprised with the first half of this chapter titled verse because the "law" is surely the major thought people have about religion, including Christianity. No surprise there. The mystery would be that Jesus significantly changed this paradigm. But He did and it is vital we know what He brought and offers us because these are the only effective "tools" for fulfilling the goal of our faith, the salvation of our souls.

   Why and how, then, is it possible are we **not** told God's great foundational Mountain truth that:

> "The law was given through Moses; **grace and truth** came through Jesus Christ" ^{Jn 1:17}

And why are we not taught what this means in practice so we can do what Jesus further says about it? If this is what Jesus brought and offers us, we should logically believe it is to help us in reaching our goal, the salvation of our souls. Otherwise, *God's Word* would simply be a mish-mash of ideas that may confuse more than enlighten us.

Again, even most regular church attendees would struggle in providing a credible answer if asked: "What, if anything new, did Jesus 'bring' His followers?" – only a very small percentage of people would quickly correctly reply (I certainly could not have answered this question for many of my early first year**s**): "Grace and truth of course!" This simply points out how poor our teaching has been on such an obvious (after told) truth. And it highlights how, once told a great Mountain truth like this, we will immediately be more confident in our faith and reading of *God's Word.*

While we have a good idea as to what truth means in general, we still need *God's Word* to clearly delineate the key truths accompanying salvation. Grace, though, is a far "fuzzier" concept. Yet, knowing this is what Jesus brought should make us far more interested in seeking and finding what grace *really* means and encompasses.

Since Jesus apparently brought "only" two things shouldn't we have a fairly good handle on them? Of course. So next, let's take a short look at Jesus' Grace.

31

7. *What is Grace?*

"The unmerited favor of God" is the most common answer given to the question: "What is Grace?" with "Huh – that's a good question" being a close runner-up. However, neither reply is very helpful.

The unmerited favor of God, while certainly true, is nonetheless a somewhat wimpy and underwhelming definition.

> Unmerited: not earned, deserved, warranted . . .

> Favor: aid, assistance . . . party favor

These don't sound all that mountainous!

Interestingly, assuming Grace is **really** such a high Mountain truth and great theme of *God's Word*, we have to wonder why it is not precisely defined in a sentence or two (or paragraph, page, chapter or even book) in *God's Word*. We, of course, are not told why, but if I had to guess it is because it is so pervasive, from cover to cover, any definition would be inadequate.

"Well," many people will surely say, "If it is true that Grace is *so* important, I certainly don't hear a lot about it in church – we used to periodically sing *Amazing Grace*, but I can't remember the last time we did − can it then really be that big, that high and majestic a truth and theme of *God's Word*?" Again, we know it must be since this is one of two great gifts Jesus brought and offers us. And the failure to clearly teach about Christ's offered Graces is maybe the greatest single sign of a loss of direction by the Church.

Without trying to state what *God's Word* doesn't delineate in a sentence or two, it is noteworthy and highly remarkable and illuminating that Grace is the <u>only</u> word that can be consistently interchanged with "Jesus," in *God's Word*, and vice versa. A very important example will demonstrate:

> *Ephesians 2:8-9* tell us: "For by <u>grace</u> you have been saved through faith, and that not of yourselves; it is the gift of God, not of works, lest anyone should boast."

But it is just as fair to say:

> For by <u>Jesus Christ</u> you have been saved through faith, and that not of yourselves; it [He] is the gift of God, not of works, lest anyone should boast.

In the previous chapter we highlighted the key verse: "The law was given through Moses; grace and truth came through Jesus Christ." And later in the book of John, Jesus says:

> "I am the way, and the truth, and the life. No one comes to the Father except through me." [Jn 14:6]

"I Am" (Jesus says), "the way, and the truth, and the life." And in the same way He can rightly say: "I Am Grace." Thus, logically answering the question as to why Grace is not defined in *God's Word*; we generally do not, nor can we, define a person. So that maybe the best way to understand Grace is to say Jesus is His Name and Grace is what He offers us and how He relates to us. In a sense, Grace is our connection to Christ. Like the proverbial penny with head and tail sides, Jesus and Grace are two (inseparable) sides of the Father's greatest of all possible gifts to us.

It is equally true that Grace (Jesus) is the key theme of *God's Word* in its entirety from *Genesis 1:1* to the end of *Revelation* – Jesus is identified as the One Who made everything that is for His and our great pleasure – this is all His Grace. Thus, any definition of Grace is inadequate for Jesus, as we see Him in His robes of Grace, is foundational to **every** Word of God given us.

Some of the confusion about Grace is certainly the result of people knowing or experiencing other religions that universally have goals and requirements that, to one degree or another, focus on what followers of that faith must do to please or appease their god – the Judeo-Christian religion (as detailed in *God's Word* – God's only Word for us) has none of this. For Christianity is the <u>only</u> religion based solely on Grace, what God does for us, not a bargain between what we supposedly do for a god now with a promise of future (after we die) blessings. We will later highlight several key Mountain verses that further make this point very powerfully, but for now we need to begin seeing the very great difference between Christianity and **all** other religions – this is Jesus/Grace.

So, in trying to provide an explanation of Grace we would probably say more by saying less:

Grace: God's Gifts for us (in their virtually infinite forms and numbers), <u>given</u> with no expectation or need of repayment by us accompanied by His appropriate disciplines necessary to guard and protect these gifts.

There are currently about 7.6 billion inhabitants of earth, enclosed on a self-contained sphere. We are together consuming monumental amounts of food and resources on a daily basis (in addition to the estimated 100 billion other people who have preceded us and since died). How does this occur? A Christian believer is going to say it is by Grace, otherwise there is no explanation that, without any outside "input" other than Grace (and sunlight, another Grace of Jesus) we are all fed and possess everything else we need and consume to live. It is not so unlike contemplating a cow in a pasture eating only grass and coming into a barn twice a day to provide milk – go figure!

And one last point before we scale other Mountain truths and verses standing in the shadow of God's Grace: let's look at the great difference between what is termed God's "Common" and His "Special" Grace.

Common Grace – The Gifts of God to all people, believers and non-believers: As the "closed sphere" concept discussed above indicates: *God's Word* says that everything we have comes by and through God's Grace. In spite of the fact that some people think they are the source of what they have we find God with a different view – two verses sum-up His thoughts:

The Father causes His sun to rise on the evil and the good, and sends rain on the righteous and the unrighteous. ^{Mt 5:45}

    You might say in your heart, "The power and strength of my hands have made this wealth for me." But remember that it is the LORD your God who gives you the power to gain wealth. ^{Du 8:17-18}

<u>Special Grace</u>, on a dramatically different hand, is the Grace of eternal salvation limited to authentic Christians (the primary focus of our review of God's Mountain verses). We are thankful for Common Grace but, ultimately, Special Grace is what we are designed for and the goal of our faith.

    Jesus/Grace is inexhaustible and often, to us humans, incomprehensible no matter how long and diligently we will study Him – which is the point of highlighting this, the Mount Everest of the great *Bible* Mountain truths and realities – everything (all other Mountain verses we look at) stand in the shadow of this great blessing and truth, "<u>Grace and truth</u> came [and comes] through Jesus Christ."

    It should be clear by now what we mentioned earlier: in as few pages as we have here it is obvious this is not going to be deep teaching. But we can hope for, in highlighting these key verses, a much greater awareness of *God's Word's* important foundational themes to whet our appetite for reading the *Bible* to see how these truth themes help make better sense of what previously may have been all "Greek" to us.

    So, let's next move to that which we are told and, therefore, for which we have no excuse for not knowing (a failure with potentially devastating eternal negative ramifications): To whom does God give His Special (eternal life-saving) Grace? (Hint: **not** to everyone, not to those who ask for it . . .). It is important to know God's Mountain truths because He is not sloppy with His truths and gifts − He tells us precisely what they are and how (<u>only</u> how) we receive, protect and retain them. In a sense, *God's Word* is a recipe book for life and, like any recipe, we should only expect a good outcome with the correct following of its instructions.

So, let's look now at the next ingredient in the salvation of our souls − to whom does God gives His Grace?

8. To Whom Does God Give Grace (Jesus)?

This is obviously not a minor theoretical issue, but likely the most important, consequential and practical truth we **must** know assuming the goal of our faith is the salvation of our souls and we are saved by Grace as *God's Word* tells us. Then why do most people who attend church week after week, year by year, not know this great Mountain truth? After all, we are told this three times in *God's Word*, once in the *Old Testament* and twice in the *New.*

Why does this question so disturb me? Because I was some years into this Christian "thing" until I clearly saw this now obvious and foundational truth. And if it were just me (with most people knowing it), I wouldn't have anyone else to be frustrated with. Or, if I had not been distracted in being taught, preached to and learning many FAR LESS important traditions and denominational distinctives I may have no beef. But when I *finally* saw this truth and mentioned it to other people, I found they didn't know it either. And it was in personal *God's Word* reading, not Church instruction, that I discovered this great truth.

And even though I eventually "got it," I wonder just how much real potential growth time was lost in discovering it years after I should have known it? And potentially what am I still missing based on a similar random and hit and miss method of church instruction? This is all *very* bewildering and frustrating!

But back to the great question and answer at hand: To whom does God give Grace?

God opposes the proud but **gives grace to the humble**. Pr 3:34, 1Pe 5:5 & Jas 4:6

Special Grace is not given (as is most often guessed), to those "who ask for it," but to (and *only* to) the humble, meaning those who admit the absolute and total impossibility on anyone's part (no matter how rich, educated, "good" . . . they are) to achieve eternal life apart from God's Special Grace **given** them. They must recognize the great personal challenge and need **and** His greater power and promise for meeting these needs with a resulting submission to Him in actively seeking His instructions to us related to this offered gift of gifts. And for further confirmation and clarity, Jesus tells and warns us (tying together the requirements of repentance and humility to be saved):

> Truly, I say to you, <u>unless you turn</u> [repent] and become like children, you will never enter the kingdom of heaven. Whoever <u>humbles</u> himself like this child is the greatest in the kingdom of heaven. Mt 18:3-4

In a sense, Jesus' great first recorded public Word, "Repent," is humility in action, a humility/repentance that begins when we are born again and continues to grow to the end of our earthly lives. Any thought we can conjure up great humility, be saved, and then effectively tell God we now don't need Him further is foolish.

Thus, we find that the great Mountain verses we have looked at so far are not disconnected and isolated Mountain truths rather they are inexorably inter-connected; the goal of our faith (the salvation of our souls), is through Grace, given only to the humble, the repenters to Jesus' truth.

Do you feel my pain and frustration?

- We are too often taught (rather than warned about conflicting with *God's Word*) traditions.
- We are not told the goal of our faith is the salvation of our souls.
- We are not clearly taught "Repent" begins with being born again, continuing until we die.
- Well over half of regular church attenders are led to believe we are saved by faith, not Grace as *God's Word* tells us.
- We have a very limited and hazy idea as to what Grace is and how it is fully linked to Jesus.
- And to top it all off, we do not know the simple (and obvious once told) vital truth that God gives grace to, and only to, the humble!

Grace is, in its fullness, incomprehensible to any of us so we are excused for not knowing all of Grace A to Z, we will be learning and experiencing it until the day we die and forever into eternity. But when simply and clearly told the great Mountain truth (to whom God gives His Grace) who would want to try to live an authentic Christian life without knowing this vital truth?

"OK, I get it, 'God gives grace to the humble,' but what, in practice and day-to-day life, does humility look like?" This is a good and important question on which our next Mountain verse sheds much light and truth.

9. *"God chose* _____*."*

"OK. Got it – God gives grace to the humble," but what does this look like in real life?" is the next great question and Mountain truth so often **not** taught and preached in church. And for the other overlooked Mountain verses we have looked at, for which the neglect is harder to explain, this great "God chose" (and still chooses . . .) Mountain truth has an obvious reason for its not being taught and preached: the simple fear of offending people.

The church has been infected with the same disease as the surrounding culture, the cult of valuing "self-esteem" above truth where "average" has become a great pejorative and insult to be avoided at all costs. In stark contrast to how *God's Word* realistically "paints" everyone, churches so often preach a message much like that of the folks living in Garrison Keller's mythical Lake Wobegon where "all the women are strong, all the men are good-looking, and all the children are above average." Much of the church doesn't want to be the "Debbie Downer" of society so they preach a similar message.

> "All . . . are good in the eyes of the LORD, and he is pleased with them." ^{Mal 2:17}

This verse points out, as we have heard, you can find a verse in *God's Word* (twisted enough) that seemingly justifies anything. If we accept this very common belief, without reading the entire verse, we might also believe (as so many in church think of themselves) that "God chose" (and continues to choose) the above average, those who work hard to do right . . . But, instead, in truth we find:

> "<u>God chose the foolish</u> things of the world to shame the wise; God chose the <u>weak</u> things of the world to shame the strong. He chose the <u>lowly</u> things of this world and the <u>despised</u> things — and the <u>things that are not</u> — to nullify the things that are, <u>so that no one may boast before him</u>."
> 1Cor 1:27-29

But without reading anything in *God's Word* other than the verse we looked at in the prior chapter (God opposes the proud but gives grace to the humble ^{Pr 3:34, 1Pe 5:5 & Jas 4:6}), we know why this was true for the Corinthians and, likewise, must still be the case for us: no matter how smart, strong, rich . . . anyone may be; unless we humble ourselves in relation to God and our fellow man, understanding just how *really* foolish, weak, poor we are, we will not see our need of, seek and take God's Grace, what Jesus came to offer us.

This great Mountain truth and key theme of *God's Word* will become increasingly obvious in view of the other great Mountain truths we will look at, but for now we must know and be frequently reminded (read for ourselves in *God's Word* if not faithfully preached in church) the great truth that God is not, like the Marines, looking for a "few good men," but for those who see and know their great need of Him and His Grace!

Likewise, as we will look at next, how frustrating is it to have not been told and taught very early on <u>where</u> (in *God's Word)* we find His best "picture" of salvation? Again, once told (yes, it sounds like a broken record), these great Mountain truths are really simple and obvious – why, then, are they not stressed in church? And probably there is no more serious case of treating "Mountains as molehills" than our not being told and taught early on <u>where</u>, in *God's Word*, we find His best "picture" of salvation. For these, little over 200 words, are certainly worth many thousands of alternate words!

   The goal of our faith is the salvation of our souls, why then are we not pointed to God's "roadmap" for this??? This is a very serious shortcoming of churches.

10. Where, in God's Word, is His Best "Picture" of Salvation
Against which we can examine ourselves to see if we are in the faith?

There are people proclaiming single salvation verses, mostly notably:

- *John 3:16* – they often do not even write out the verse in words it is so commonly known by its verse reference.
- If you confess with your mouth that Jesus is Lord and believe in your heart that God raised him from the dead, you will be saved. ^{Ro 10:9}

Of course, these are great verses and truths. But **they are not <u>the</u> "go to" and comprehensive salvation Mountain teachings** of ***God's Word*** – for that we have to read ***Ephesians 2:1-10*** (with *John 3:16, Romans 10:9* and other great complementary verses supporting this "major" explanation and delineation of the salvation process).

> As for you, **you were dead** in your transgressions and sins, in which you used to live when you followed the ways of this world and of the ruler of the kingdom of the air, the spirit who is now at work in those who are disobedient. **All of us** also lived among them at one time, gratifying the cravings of our flesh and following its desires and thoughts. Like the rest, we **were by nature deserving of wrath**. **But** because of his great love for us, **God**, who is rich in mercy, **made us alive with Christ** even when we were dead in transgressions – **it is by**

grace you have been saved. And God raised us up with Christ and seated us with him in the heavenly realms in Christ Jesus, in order that in the coming ages he might show the incomparable riches of his grace, expressed in his kindness to us in Christ Jesus. For **it is by grace you have been saved, through faith – and this is not from yourselves, it is the gift of God** – not by works, so that no one can boast. **For we are God's handiwork, created in Christ Jesus to do good works, which God prepared in advance for us to do**.

There is a lot of meat on these bones – and as only God can do, in a few short sentences, He reveals a clear outline of His magnificent plan of salvation. As we consider and begin to understand His plan more, other Mountain passages and verses will fill in this salvation mosaic.

So let's start with a brief overview of what this Mountain truth teaches us, just how many boxes of salvation these 10 verses tick:

As for you, **you were dead** in your transgressions and sins, in which you used to live when you followed the ways of this world and of the ruler of the kingdom of the air, the spirit who is now at work in those who are disobedient. **All of us** also lived among them at one time, gratifying the cravings of our sinful nature and following its desires and thoughts. Like the rest, **we were by nature objects of wrath**.

- This verse is personal – opening with "As for **you** . . ." and confirming it applies to "All of us . . ."

- The great truth that, as Jesus says, "You must be born again" is explained in greater detail early in *Romans*:

    "As it is written [in the Psalms]:
      'There is **no one** righteous, not even one;
        there is **no one** who understands,
          no one who seeks God.
        All have turned away,
          they have together become worthless;
        there is **no one** who does good,
          not even one.'" Ro 3:10-12

As a result, "we were by nature objects of wrath. But because of his great love for us, God, who is rich in mercy, made us alive with Christ even when we were dead in transgressions."

"We love because he first loved us" 1Jn 4:19 with anything taught otherwise being a false gospel.

- "We were dead" and God "made us alive" because of His personal and particular love for those He saves, not because of anything we could or would do – we were dead and dead people don't "decide to," "accept" or have a will to do anything!

- Salvation is "to Christ," with these verses also showing where and what we are saved "from." We must know our poor, lost and desperate condition to see and seek salvation from spiritual death "to Christ" – repent in humility to Christ, with increasing repentance over the succeeding months and years being, in essence, humility in action.

And at this point, in our impossibly lost condition, God makes "us alive with Christ;" **He** saves us.

It is <u>by Grace</u> you have been saved. And God raised us up with Christ and seated us with him in the heavenly realms in Christ Jesus, in order that in the coming ages he might show the incomparable riches of his Grace, expressed in his kindness to us in Christ Jesus.

- Wow, as we have said, Grace is very important and special because God saves His redeemed by Grace "in order that in the coming ages he might show the incomparable riches of his Grace." God's highest Grace for man is "expressed in his kindness to us in Christ Jesus," in saving us.

For **it is by Grace you have been saved, <u>through</u> faith** – and this not from yourselves, it is the gift of God – not by works, so that no one can boast.

- And we must be very susceptible to forgetting **we are saved by Grace** since God feels it necessary to repeat it a second time in this short passage.

- Likewise, God must have understood it was important to re-emphasize that "it is by Grace you have been saved . . . not by works, so that no one can boast" because of man's tendency to sing our own praises even about what we are given. God is here reminding us that, before salvation, we were dead, without hope or there being anything, as a dead person, we could meaningfully do to be saved.

- Said a third way, even the faith through (not "by") which we are saved, is not something we had but, is a "gift of God." People very often fail to make the proper distinction between our natural and very limited pre-Grace faith and the Grace-faith special "gift of God." Everyone has faith, but only those gifted with God's Grace-faith will have the faith required to be saved. Again, *Romans 3* (and *Romans 9*) explain this aspect of God's salvation in a complementary and more detailed manner. And this Grace-faith is not just a *New Testament* phenomenon; we find in the *Old Testament* the same truth – true spiritual faith (in contrast to "natural" faith) has always been from God:

  "To this day the LORD has not given you a mind that understands or eyes that see or ears that hear." ^{Deu 29:4}

 For we are God's workmanship, created in Christ Jesus to do good works, which God prepared in advance for us to do.

- With this last sentence, of this great Mountain passage, telling us the "for" (God's expectation) of our salvation.
- We should not be surprised by His telling us: "we are God's workmanship, created in Christ Jesus" since this is a reiteration and summary of what we have been told in the nine previous verses.
- What, however, will likely shock most people reading and contemplating this passage (even those attending church for many years) is that "we are . . . created . . . to do good works, which God prepared in advance for us to do."

 As the clear consummation of this great Mountain range of verses it is unbelievable how the "for" of God's salvation is so routinely overlooked and treated as a molehill. We now know the "goal of our faith is the salvation of our souls." In a sense, the goal (and certainly a great truth that must be present in any self-examination to see if we are in the faith) is the resulting (or lack of in the case of a false profession of faith) "good works, which God prepared in advance for us to do."

 This is certainly no molehill, so we have to wonder and ask ourselves: How in the world could this great salvation punch line be so often overlooked and minimized?

We are saved:

- **FROM** death in our transgressions and sins, in which all of us used to live when we followed the ways of this world and of the ruler of the kingdom of the air, the spirit who is now at work in those who are disobedient.
- **BECAUSE of** God's great love and mercy for us.
- **TO** life with Christ.
- **BY** "Grace."
- **IN ORDER THAT** in the coming ages he might show the incomparable riches of his grace, expressed in his kindness to us in Christ Jesus.
- **THROUGH** faith – this is not from yourselves, it is the gift of God.
- **NOT by** works, so that no one can boast.
- **FOR** we are God's handiwork, created in Christ Jesus to do good works, which God prepared in advance for us to do.

So, it all comes together into God's very straightforward "plan of salvation" ONCE we reject the opinions and ideas of men, their traditions and denominational distinctives:

- ✓ Jesus warned, "You have a fine way of rejecting the commandment of God in order to establish your traditions!"
- ✓ God's clearly defined "goal of our faith is the salvation of your souls."
- ✓ The first recorded public Word of Jesus is "Repent" – repent from the world to Christ.
- ✓ "The law was given through Moses; grace and truth came through Jesus Christ"
- ✓ Grace is Christ and all He does for us, the highlight being our eternal salvation.
- ✓ God gives this Special (salvation) Grace to the humble.
- ✓ *Ephesians 2:1-10* is God's best "picture" of salvation.

   Maybe an analogy will help make the point about the importance of God's Mountain verses. *God's Word* is more like Switzerland than Holland. While both are beautiful countries, you do not go to Holland to see mountains, for this you go to Switzerland. *God's Word* is "built" around major Mountain verses with lesser supporting truths, stories, examples . . . provided to complement these great truths; to neglect the high Mountains is to miss most of what God is trying to show and tell us. Failing to see and appreciate these greater verses and themes explains much of the reason people stop trying to read *God's Word* – while, on the other hand, seeing these great truths makes *God's Word* more understandable, practical and thus interesting, rich and compelling.

All of which still leaves us with the next big question: What is the #1 foundational good work God planned for <u>all</u> Christians? Is there a single common good work for all authentic Christians? Are we told? Yes, and again simply and clearly. But need we ask yet again: "Why are we are not told?" It is not as if any of these questions/answers are "deep," theoretical and ethereal; quite the opposite, they are simple and obvious once we are shown them!

We certainly need to know what Jesus tells us "The work of God is . . ." It would be interesting to ask **any** pastor their excuse for **all** his regular attenders not knowing this; after all, hasn't **every** authentic Christian had the desire to know "What does God **most** want me to do?"

11. Jesus says: "The work of God is _____."

We are told in *Ephesians 2:1-9* the process of salvation and in verse 10 the "for" of our salvation:

> For we are God's handiwork, created in Christ Jesus to do good works, which God prepared in advance for us to do.

It is both discouraging and baffling we are not taken to the very top of this great Mountain verse to learn what it shows us about life's greatest possible goal and its fulfillment: the salvation of our souls. It is disheartening *until* we realize it is a fairly common reality, we probably aren't going to be taught the great Mountain truths of *God's Word* in church so we must take personal responsibility for reading and finding them ourselves!

There is clearly another enlightening Mountain verse we *must* also know if we take our faith seriously – Jesus in a single sentence unequivocally tells us the "work of God is . . .," yet we are not taught this. We have to compare this with some of the molehill messages we hear in church and just scratch our heads wondering what is going on? Sadly, too often denominational differences and traditions obscure these great Mountain truths. For who could deny, when we are told by Jesus: "The work of God is . . .," any authentic and serious Christian would not be eager to know this very very important truth?

> Jesus says, "The work of God is this: **to believe in the One He has sent**." Jn 6:29

Jesus is talking to a large crowd and, at one point, says:

> "**Do not work for food that spoils, but for food that endures to eternal life**, which the Son of Man will **give** [Grace] you. For on him God the Father has placed his seal of approval."
>
> Then they asked him, "What must we do to do the works God requires?"
>
> Jesus answered, "The work of God is this: to believe in the one he has sent." ^{Jn 6: 27-29}

Neither they nor we then have a legitimate reason for not knowing (and certainly preachers have even less excuse for not presenting) this as the very great and high Mountain truth it obviously is.

Why would this be the work of God? Obviously because we are saved by Grace through faith, "without faith it is impossible to please God" ^{Heb 11:6} and "the goal of our faith is the salvation of our souls." Faith is, in a sense, simply taking the Grace Jesus offers us.

And it does not take much thought to realize "the work of God" is a double entendre – Jesus is stating this here as a theme of two important and cooperative trains of thought:

1. The work God does, before we can do anything, in giving us Grace-faith (faith beyond any man's natural faith).
2. What we do with this Grace-faith: the personal and specific "assigned" good works, not some generic list of good works or even good works we dream up –

these are the exact and precise good works God prepared in advance for us
individually to do in our remaining earthly life, however long or short.
Without both works no one is saved.

Grace, in its many and frequent forms, is the "umbrella" work of God that He does for us "to believe in the One He has sent" for, as we are told in *Ephesians 2,* "It is by grace you have been saved, through faith – and this is not from yourselves, it is the gift of God – not by [our - man's] works, so that no one can boast."

Elsewhere, as just two of many verses sitting in the shadow and supporting this great Mountain verse, we find:

> He [God the Father] who began a good <u>work</u> in you will carry it on to completion until the day of Christ Jesus. Phil 1:6

> <u>Continue to work</u> out your salvation with fear and trembling, <u>for it is God who works in you</u> to will and to act in order to fulfill his good purpose. Phil 2:12-13

Armed and supported by all that God, in His Grace, offers to give us, we must not be distracted and waylaid from the great goal of our faith, indeed the great goal of life, the salvation of our souls:

> "Do not work for food that spoils, but for food that endures to eternal life, <u>which the Son of Man will give you</u>."

We aren't even to work for food to eat Jesus tells us – we have to, with sole focus, continue to work out our salvation with fear and trembling.

God's Word is always reminding us (in reality, we are to be listening as the Holy Spirit reminds us through *God's Word*) of what Jesus told us, "The work of God is this: to believe in the One He has sent." As we do this it is vital to know and remember:

- Our very practical work (the "good works He prepared in advance for us to do") necessary to achieving the goal of our faith.
- God is also working for the same goal and is our real hope and surety of accomplishing it, reminding us of the great rhetorical question: "If God is for us, who can be against us?" [Ro 8:31] We cannot lose with God leading and protecting us – we ARE going to finish our life's key work of believing in His Son and all He has done, is doing and will do for us in this work!

But this still leaves us with the big question of how we are to know God's *specific* will for us? Not surprisingly, from a key Mountain verse that, while sometimes mentioned in church, has been in decline and now routinely dismissed altogether or treated as a relative molehill, not the great Mountain truth and reality it is.

12. The Word of God is _____.

"All Scripture is God-breathed and is useful for teaching, rebuking, correcting and training in righteousness, **so that** the man of God may be thoroughly equipped <u>for every good work</u>." 2 Tim 3:16-17 — good works planned in advance for us to do.

You have been born again, not of perishable seed, but of imperishable, **through the living and enduring word of God**." 1Pe 1:23

Faith comes from hearing, and hearing **through the word of Christ**. Ro 10:17

Once we see these great truths it is obvious how the Mountain verses we have previously looked at so perfectly fit together and support each other.

In contrast, who could deny that we are in an age of strong and vocal opinions? Opinions are appealing because they require no logic, no hard work in thinking and no second guessing. "In my opinion . . ." is the new Gold Standard of decision-making. Opinion polls rule in politics as well as public and private ethics.

Under this banner of freedom of opinions even those labeling themselves "Christian" espouse dramatically differing "Christian" messages and doctrines:

- Pro-life ~ Pro-Choice?
- Unmarried living together?
- God in favor of or opposed to same sex marriage?

- Democrat ~ Republican?

No problem. On one subject after another we can find "good" Christians and Christian Churches having diametrically opposing opinions. But on one point they do agree: they are speaking for God, of this they are confident.

 In this conflicting reality, reference to *God's Word* is increasingly unthinkable or secondary at best. Many church-goers will freely claim the *Bible* is the Word of God and then hypocritically and inexplicably not read or seek to live it.

   Fast forward to life's end and the concept of meeting God in heaven: if He asks, "Why didn't you read my Word (my <u>only</u> written and personal Word to you)," how/what will we answer? Do we *really* think God will be sitting of the edge of His throne excited about hearing our opinions?

- "I had better things to do with my time."
- "I simply did not have time with my other, more pressing, responsibilities."
- "I tried to read it, but found your Word too boring or incomprehensible."
- "I didn't want to know what I might read in it because I considered you hard and demanding and, as a result, my ignorance was bliss."
- "Nobody (my preacher included) placed much, if any, emphasis in the necessity of reading it."

- "It is *so* old I didn't consider it possibly relevant in the 21st Century."
- "_____ " ← fill in the blank if you can think of a better reason.
- Bottom-line: "I really didn't care what you had to tell me!"

What do you think will be a legitimate response for which God will reply: "Yes, you are very right – I can see it was better for you to 'wing' life rather than read and give thought to what I have to say."

If God had provided us a large library detailing His thoughts we *might* have *some* excuse for not knowing where to start, much less finish with this task. If, whatever He provided, was merely ancient thoughts of thousands of years ago, if *God's Word* contained known errors, such that we had no confidence of what was right or wrong in it, if it was written beyond a child's ability to comprehend what it said, if it were all about theoretical and "religious" ideas or if, indeed, its writers (including Jesus) stated "In my opinion . . ." in their writings we could legitimately claim being confused about reading it. But God clearly tells us, in a great Mountain verse:

> "The word of God is <u>living and active</u>, sharper than any two-edged sword, piercing to the division of soul and of spirit, of joints and of marrow, and discerning the thoughts and intentions of the heart." Heb 4:12

As we saw, in a prior key Mountain verse:

> "The law was given through Moses; grace and truth came through Jesus Christ" Jn 1:17

This truth is His Word!

Likewise, as we have highlighted in another (sadly seldom taught) Mountain verse:

> For we are God's handiwork, created in Christ Jesus to do good works, which God prepared in advance for us to do. Eph 2:10

This being true, God *must* communicate His wishes to us somehow, some way. And He does so in many ways, with His Word being the final "fact-checker" to discern His Voice from the many other voices speaking to us all the time from many directions. Against *God's Word* we are told to:

> Test everything; hold on to the good. 1Thes 5:21

Everything including others' good counsel and opinions, even what preachers tell us – we are personally responsible for testing everything because God has exact, unique, precise and personal good works for every Christian to do with His Word, His "living and active, sharper than any two-edged sword, piercing . . ." Word as our *necessary* guide. As Jesus requested of God the Father:

> "Sanctify them by the truth; your word is truth." Jn 17:17

Sanctification representing the "salvation of our souls" from the time of being born again until and through our time on earth ends.

God's Word isn't just lucky to have a few good thoughts that we are calling Mountain verses – it is a fountain of help in an otherwise bleak terrain of helplessness from worldly "wisdom" (really just opinions).

God is more serious about His Word than we are – this should not be!

> "If anyone is ashamed of me and my words [Jesus speaking], the Son of Man will be ashamed of him when he comes in his glory and in the glory of the Father and of the holy angels." Lk 9:26

In just one chapter of *God's Word* (admittedly the longest, *Psalm 119*), God relates a few of the important blessings of His Word:

- I rejoice in following your statutes as one rejoices in **great riches**.
- Your statutes are my delight; they are **my counselors**.
- My soul is weary with sorrow; **strengthen me** according to your word.
- Great **peace** have they who love your law, and nothing can make them stumble.
- Direct me in the path of your commands, for there I find **delight**.
- I will walk about in **freedom**, for I have sought out your precepts.
- I remember your ancient laws, O LORD, and I find **comfort** in them.
- The law from your mouth is **more precious to me than thousands of pieces of silver and gold**.

- I have put **my hope** in your word.
- May my heart be blameless toward your decrees, **that I may not be put to shame**.
- Your word, O LORD, is **eternal; it stands firm in the heavens**.
- If your law had not been my delight, I would have perished in my affliction. I will never forget your precepts, for **by them you have preserved my life**.
- To all perfection I see a limit; but **your commands are boundless**.
- **Your commands make me wiser than my enemies** . . . for they are ever with me.
- **I have more insight than all my teachers**, for I meditate on your statutes.
- **I have more understanding than the elders**, for I obey your precepts.
- It **gives understanding to the simple**.
- Your word is **a lamp to my feet and a light for my path**.
- **Your statutes are wonderful**.
- **How sweet are your words** to my taste, sweeter than honey to my mouth!

- Your promises have been thoroughly tested, and **your servant loves them**.
- **Oh, how I love your law!**
- **May my lips overflow with praise, for you teach me your decrees.**
- **May my tongue sing of your word, for all your commands are righteous.**
- May your hand be ready to help me, for I have chosen your precepts.
- May **your laws sustain me**.

Have we experienced these blessings? Have we even sought them? Only in developing a discipline of reading *God's Word* will we find its very real benefits as God intends.

Our personal view of, and the value we place in, *God's Word*? The sure trend in people reading *God's Word* (and preachers preaching it!) is certainly a downward trajectory and this at a time it is of greater importance to read it <u>more</u> and preach it even <u>more</u> faithfully. As the world draws further away from God, His followers must pull further away from the world, submitting themselves <u>more</u> to God, with greater attention to His Word being necessary to "cleanse" us from the increasingly oppressive and misleading voices of the world. The Word of God is never optional, and in times of decline (as we certainly currently see and can feel the "foundations being destroyed" [Ps 11:3]) *God's Word* becomes increasingly important.

That this great truth is being minimized IN CHURCH is unbelievable. But this simply reminds us that faith is personal, salvation is personal, we are responsible personally for Whom we choose to listen to. The only eternally safe route, achieved in life, is the choice Joshua made:

> "If serving the LORD seems undesirable to you, then choose for yourselves this day whom you will serve . . . But as for me and my household, we will serve the LORD." Jos 24:15

And this is not possible apart from reading *God's Word* and it then being our foundation! And this is a footing of Good News we would know if we were taught another great Mountain truth that . . .

13. *Missing the Grace and Beauty of a Great & Important Mountain Truth*

Like traveling a long distance to see a great mountain, only to do so on a rainy foggy day, is much like the way a well-known and beloved (not so much today, but in the past) passage is now taught, if preached at all:

> And now, Israel [today's Christian] what does the Lord your God ask of you but to fear the Lord your God, to walk in obedience to him, to love him, to serve the Lord your God with all your heart and with all your soul, and to observe the Lord's commands and decrees that I am giving you today . . . Dt 10:12-13

For they leave off teaching the beautiful peak (the last four words) of this great Mountain truth, a truth very important to understanding much of the rest of *God's Word*. Not highlighting this is about like, in preaching *Ephesians 2:1-9,* explaining *how* we are saved while leaving out the "for" of our salvation: "for we are God's handiwork, created in Christ Jesus to do good works, which God prepared in advance for us to do" or never explaining the goal of our faith, the salvation of our souls.

> "What does the Lord your God ask of you but to fear the Lord your God, to walk in obedience to him, to love him, to serve the Lord your God with all your heart and with all your soul, and to observe the Lord's commands and decrees that I am giving you today

for your own good?"

There is not a SINGLE command in *God's Word* that is NOT for our own good. Being taught and understanding this is the basis for eagerly desiring to find and know <u>all</u> God says and promises in His Word rather than dreading to find what He says next.

Overcoming Maybe the Biggest Lie and Strategy of the Devil

The underlying attitude that "caught" Adam and Eve and still works best today to undermine faith? When we hear and follow the evil voices leading us, like a teenager, to chaff under the supposed onerous rules of God and, as a result, seek what we want when we want it.

A simple story of Jesus, from *God's Word*, may best highlight this very common feeling:

> Jesus proceeded to tell them a parable . . . "A man of noble birth went to a distant country to lay claim to his kingship and then return. Beforehand, he called ten of his servants and gave them ten minas. 'Conduct business with this until I return,' he said . . .When he returned from procuring his kingship, he summoned the servants to whom he had given the money, to find out what each one had earned . . .
>
> "The first one came and said, 'Sir, your mina has earned ten more.' . . . The second came and said, 'Sir, your mina has earned five more . . .' Then another servant came and said, 'Master, here is your mina, which I have laid away in a piece of cloth. For I was

67

afraid of you, because you are a harsh man. You withdraw what you did not deposit and reap what you did not sow.'

"His master replied, 'You wicked servant, I will judge you by your own words. So you knew that I am a harsh man, withdrawing what I did not deposit and reaping what I did not sow?'" Lk 19:11-22

This last man voiced the most common impression of God as one who is hard and demanding. Sadly, the last servant missed the "memo" (because He failed to read *God's Word*!) that *everything* in *God's Word* is for our own good – he was listening, instead, to some religious traditions of man that are based on our supposed self-sacrifice for God, not God's Grace for us. So he falsely assumed God is a "harsh man. You withdraw what you did not deposit and reap what you did not sow," which is simply rejection and blasphemy of God.

To be free to *want* to read *God's Word*, we must consciously know and return to this Mountain verse and remember, <u>everything</u> God tells us to do/not to do is for our good – our freedom.

"Well," some may say, "What about the many commandments 'do this . . .' 'don't do that . . .?'" In response, we simply have to ask: "Which is for other than **_our own_** good?" Certainly not God's prohibitions against murder, adultery, lying, stealing . . .

Of course, there are many verses in *God's Word* associated with what we must do and not do, but these are all of greater blessing to us than "doing our own thing." We are always blessed in doing what God tells us to do (and not doing what will hurt us).

God's Word certainly has some very great dos and don'ts requiring great repentances. We, then, choose to read some great commands of God with an accent on what we have to do or as they are written for us to read, what God gives us, how He blesses us, as we live a life that most benefits us, **always for our own good**.

Certainly, the greatest challenges of God (requiring us to set aside **everything** for the sake of Christ and necessary for achieving the goal of our faith, the salvation of our souls) are impossible without God's Grace-faith, but even here Jesus promises:

> "I tell you the truth, no one who has left home or wife or brothers or parents or children for the sake of the kingdom of God will fail to receive <u>many times as much in this age</u> and, in the age to come, eternal life." Lk 18:29-30

There are verses in *God's Word*, considered apart from His specified goal of our faith, that may seem to imply that God considers man nothing and all we do/don't do has nothing to do with "our own good." For example:

> Whatever you do, in word or deed, do it all in the name of the Lord Jesus, giving thanks to God the Father through Him. Col 3:17
>
> Whatever you do, work at it with all your heart, as working for the Lord, not for human masters. Col 3:23
>
> Whether you eat or drink or whatever you do, do it all to the glory of God. 1Cor 10:31

69

Yet, God is the perfect Father and as the Creator, He does not need or want anything from us, but **gives** us everything we need to grow up and properly mature. We know we can **always**:

> Hope in God, who richly provides us with everything for our enjoyment. [1Ti 6:17]

God at no point or time *ever* increases His Glory at our expense – His Glory and our good never conflict as we keep in mind:

> Everything for God's glory is for our good and everything for our good is for God's glory.

Thus, to meet and overcome the trials and challenges of life, we must know everything, always, that God tells is **for our own good**. And this is similarly necessary as motivation to eagerly and consistently live in the love of Jesus, our next, all-too-often overlooked Mountain verse required for finishing life's race, purpose and ultimate goal, the eternal salvation of our souls.

We are so accustomed to the bad news of the world we cannot, apart from God's Grace-faith, see and enjoy the always Good News of His Word.

14. Jesus says: "If you love me, you will _____."

There may be a nut somewhere who might irrationally say we don't have to love Jesus if we expect to ultimately achieve the goal of our faith, the glorification and eternal salvation of our souls. But the vast majority of people would recognize this as foolish. Yet, sadly, most would not be able to complete the last half of this great Mountain verse:

Jesus says: "If you love me, <u>you will keep my commandments</u>." Jn 14:15

Not knowing God's great Mountain passages offers openings of attack by satan – and he certainly takes advantage of our ignorance of this verse and the other unknown Mountain truths we have looked at.

Certainly, "you will keep my commandments" *presumes* we are "in" His Word. We are the ones who turn our backs on Christ – walking away from His Word and love, or more rightly said, feeling we have enough of Him to get by and turn back to the world for our supposed fulfillment. But love is not a stagnant or one-time event, thus Jesus also tells us:

"**Remain** in me, and I will **remain** in you. No branch can bear fruit by itself; it must **remain** in the vine. Neither can you bear fruit unless you **remain** in me.

"I am the vine; you are the branches. If a man **remains** in me and I in him, he will bear much fruit; **apart from me you can do nothing**. If anyone does not **remain** in me, he is like a branch that is thrown away and withers; such branches are picked up, thrown into the fire and burned. If you **remain** in me **<u>and my words remain in you</u>,** ask whatever you wish, and it will be given you. This is to my Father's glory, that you bear much fruit, showing yourselves to be my disciples.

   "As the Father has loved me, so have I loved you. Now **remain** in my love. If you obey my commands, you will **remain** in my love." Jn 15:4-10

"If you **remain** in me and my words **remain** in you . . ." – any thought we will know His Words and they will remain in us, based on a little time hearing it preached on Sunday, is irrational! We can only hope to grow in God's Grace, faith and love of Christ as we remain in (regularly read) His Word. And instead of an attitude of "how much do I need to read every day," we should be frustrated we cannot read and digest more!

"The word of God is living and active," every word of it is "for your own good." To remain in Christ and His love requires we are in His Word to know and fulfill the "for" of our salvation, the "good works prepared in advance for us to do!"

"But where in *God's Word* will I read of these exact 'good works prepared in advance for me precisely and specifically to do?'" This is a great question and the short answer is we won't, but knowing *God's Word* better and better is the foundation for another MIA (missing in action) great Mountain verse seldom taught or preached (and often preached against because apparently the preacher doesn't believe nor has experienced or seen it and its great glory).

15. "_____, *if you hear his voice,* _____."

"I wish I knew what God wanted me to do." "If I knew what God wanted me to do I would certainly do it." Who hasn't had these, and similar, thoughts at some time in the past? But there are debates, within Christian circles, about whether, and if so how, God speaks today. His Word certainly gives us some clear guidelines on this issue.

For to highlight just the few Mountain verses we have looked at thus far we find:

- "We are God's workmanship, created in Christ Jesus to do good works, which God prepared in advance for us to do." So, it *should* go without saying that if God created exact and precise good works for each and every Christian, He must somehow communicate His plans to them – He must somehow "speak" to them.
- "The work of God is this: to believe in the One He has sent" – this being the case, again He must show and tell us how this is accomplished on a practical daily basis.
- "The word of God is living and active" – necessarily meaning He speaks to us now through His Word.
- If told He gives us commands and decrees "today for your own good" we can expect to hear Him today.

So, not only (if we consider ourselves Christians) can we expect to hear God from time to time, we must be hearing Him frequently, daily. And this is confirmed by an *Old Testament*

Mountain verse repeated and expounded several times in the *New Testament*:

Today, if you hear his voice, do not harden your hearts. Ps 95:7-11, Heb 3:7-19 & 4:1-8

As we said in our first chapter:

"If we (personally or corporately) cancel God's Word we effectively correspondingly cancel God in our lives. For only in and through His Word do we find what God has to say to us, it being the means through which He trains us to hear His Voice and to distinguish between His Voice and the many other, often much louder, competing voices we hear all around us. God's Word is His only written Word given us. So, if God's Word falls on deaf ears and unresponsive hearts, we have effectually cancelled Him in our lives!

Happily, though, there are still large numbers of people who have not cancelled God and His Word and their testimony is that He still speaks and, in contrast to the increasingly louder more radical opposing voices, He speaks in His Word more clearly than ever. Canceling by many has counter-intuitively become a great blessing to those who have been awakened like Jesus' historic disciples to His questioning if they intended on leaving (canceling) Him as so many others were:

"Lord, to whom shall we go? You have the words of eternal life. We have come to believe and to know that you are the Holy One of God." Jn 6:66-69

God and the cancelling of His Word is (as it always has been) a largely personal matter.

74

Little has really changed. For God's Word warns us literally thousands of times and in many ways as one of its top themes that we must always personally (churches are not saved, individuals are!) remain vigilant and CAREFUL to keep God's Word real and active in our lives."

Consistently reading *God's Word* then is the primary means of hearing God's Voice – His promises, warnings, leadings, direction . . . to "remain" in Christ and hear and know His Voice for what we need to being doing NOW.

Today, if you hear his voice . . .

is a vital Mountain verse that sadly we were seldom told or taught – we MUST be in *God's Word* TODAY to hear His Voice.

16. _____ *Jesus warns: "how then will you believe if I speak of heavenly things?"*

The common caricature of Jesus, the *Bible*, "spiritual" matters . . . is that they are theoretical and ethereal (about and for when we die), anything but practical and for now. And very sadly, this viewpoint is only reinforced for many people by what they hear in church.

Against this backdrop, what then can we make of Jesus' rhetorical question in *John 3*:

> "I have spoken to you of earthly things and you do not believe; how then will you believe if I speak of heavenly things?" Jn 3:12

What 'earthly things' is He talking about? We claim a saving faith we can't reasonably define or support and we feel we are pleasing God with this faith and confidently rest assured we will be ok when we die without the slightest idea of what this means for the here and now (other than maybe just trying to be a little nicer and avoid the so-called big sins).

In man's plan, we are seemingly saved ("born again") and then, within all our current responsibilities of life, we must add a spiritual dimension to our other many existing, pressing and more "real" tasks of life.

Yet unlike what we are so often taught, **God's Word majors on earthly things as a necessary precursor, foundation and growth into a greater and greater faith in heavenly**

things. For example:

> The hand of the Lord was with them, and a large number who believed turned to the Lord. The news about them reached the ears of the church at Jerusalem, and they sent Barnabas to Antioch. When he arrived and saw **the evidence of the grace of God**, he was glad and encouraged them all to remain true to the Lord with all their hearts. Acts 11:21-23

> "Whoever lives by the truth comes into the light, so that it may be **seen plainly** that what he has done has been done through God." Jn 3:21

This last verse in the same chapter as our "earthly things" quote of Jesus.

Where, today, do we see or hear about any "evidence of the grace of God" or plainly see anything that is done as being "done through God?" And what do we do when there is a "gap" between what we think and hear in church and *God's Word?* We spiritualize, traditionalize, motivationalize, ritualize it, talk and sing about God . . . anything and everything *except* being serious about Him in 167 of our 168 hours a week! The thought of "Christ" and "practical" (earthly things) in the same sentence simply doesn't compute! The idea of "evidence" and "seen plainly" related to the things of God is something we simply cannot conceive of.

We fail to consider, though, in being very sensible and practical that the greatest and most powerful "earthly things" are intangible and even more vital to a meaningful and happy life than the tangible. For example: love, joy, peace, patience, kindness, goodness, faithfulness, gentleness, and self-control, [Gal 5: 22-23] speaking the truth in love [Eph 4:15] praise, praying . . . So why are we seldom told or pointed to where to find these earthly blessings, truths, commands and warnings and our personal responsibility in pursuing them? We are not being rightly told we are saved for a 24/7/365 Master/servant relationship with God, that "we are God's handiwork, created in Christ Jesus to do good works, which God prepared in advance for us to do." This is no part-time job!

   But how can this be? How can we be fully "engaged" with Christ when we have great practical and personal responsibilities requiring our attention? We will never know what Jesus is speaking to us here related to "earthly things" if not properly told and taught in church **and** if we are not, ourselves, in a personal quest for God's Voice and in His Word finding and living the next neglected (as just one "earthly things" example) Mountain truth we will look at.

   God's Word is in fact not simply practical it is both super- and supra-practical, above and beyond anything we are able in ourselves to see much less do! It is by Grace, accomplished ONLY by Grace-faith, supported by strong evidence that will be plainly seen when it is lived. Oh! So this explains why we don't hear about the "earthly things" of Jesus, they require impossible faith, a faith not only to "be in" Christ now but as a basis, and only foundation, for "being in" Him eternally.

   And probably nowhere, in *God's Word,* do we so clearly see the dichotomy between what Christ promises us (within the first few minutes of the *New Testament)* versus what we are taught IN CHURCH, and how we live, than in our next Mountain verse!

> "I have spoken to you of earthly things and you do not believe; how then will you believe if I speak of heavenly things?" Jn 3:12

We won't until we humble ourselves to Him and His Word above our traditions and rituals which can leave us dead to Him now and forever.

17. "_____, and all these things will be given to you as well."

What things is Jesus here speaking of? The "earthly things" (the practical necessities) of life, ALL of them! Are we told this great promise of Jesus in church? Nope. Yet Jesus, boldly, clearly and simply **promises** us He will **give** us all these things. Meaning if this promise does not come true then we can have no great faith in Jesus for anything. However, if this very great "earthly things" promise does "work," then we can have much faith in Him about heavenly things as well. This is a very pivotal verse for our faith!

> "Therefore I tell you, do not worry about your life, what you will eat or drink; or about your body, what you will wear. Is not life more than food, and the body more than clothes? Look at the birds of the air; they do not sow or reap or store away in barns, and yet your heavenly Father feeds them. Are you not much more valuable than they? Can any one of you by worrying add a single hour to your life?

> "And why do you worry about clothes? See how the flowers of the field grow. They do not labor or spin. Yet I tell you that not even Solomon in all his splendor was dressed like one of these. If that is how God clothes the grass of the field, which is here today and tomorrow is thrown into the fire, will he not much more clothe you – you of little faith? So **do not worry, saying, 'What shall we eat?' or 'What shall we drink?' or**

'What shall we wear?' For the pagans run after all these things, and your heavenly Father knows that you need them. <u>But seek first his kingdom and his righteousness</u>, and all these things will be given to you as well.</u>" Mt 6:25:33

And He prefaced this great promise by telling us:

> "Do not store up for yourselves treasures on earth, where moths and vermin destroy, and where thieves break in and steal. But store up for yourselves treasures in heaven . . .
>
> "No one can serve two masters. Either you will hate the one and love the other, or you will be devoted to the one and despise the other. You cannot serve both God and money." Mt 6:19-24

But none of this should surprise us, for we earlier saw the <u>exact</u> same promise of Jesus:

> "Do not work for food that spoils, but for food that endures to eternal life, <u>which the Son of Man will **give** you</u>. For on him God the Father has placed his seal of approval."
>
> Then they asked him, "What must we do to do the works God requires?"
>
> Jesus answered, "The work of God is this: to believe in the one he has sent." Jn 6:27-29

A related, too often disregarded, great *God's Word* truth is that (as indicated in the last Mountain verse we reviewed), we are not effectively being told the truth that we are saved for a 24/7/365 Master/servant relationship with God: "For it is by grace you have been saved, through faith — and this is not from yourselves, it is the gift of God — not by works, so that no one can boast. For we are God's handiwork, created in Christ Jesus to do good works, which God prepared in advance for us to do." This is no part-time job! It is a full-time "job" and, as such, God <u>must</u> give us everything we need if we are to do it.

Jesus obligates Himself in *Matthew 6:33* to **give** us ALL that we require for life and to fulfill His (as our Master) personally assigned good works, which He prepared in advance of our salvation, that we do. This is confirmed elsewhere in *God's Word:*

> God is able to bless you abundantly, so that in all things at all times [24/7/365], having all that you need, you will abound in every <u>good work</u>. 2Cor 9:8

Again, clear "earthly things" promises.

This promise is seldom pointed out to people, but when it is they will often foolishly reply: "You mean, then, we don't have to work?" Of course we do, doing the "good works, which God prepared in advance for us to do" is the hardest possible work – it is completed only by and through much of God's Grace.

And to this end, in God-fashion, He rewards what He provides. God gives Grace and to the extent we take and use this Grace He rewards us more and further. But this shouldn't surprise us, because this is exactly what good parents do for their children: reward them for doing what is best for them and providing further for them in the future.

This promise of Christ **giving** us everything is the basis for the largely forgotten "Stewardship" truth principle that everything and everyone is God's and we are responsible for being good servants in our use of His Grace (our time and all He gives us to accomplish the "good works, which God prepared in advance for us to do") – the "all-in" of an authentic Christian life.

In our last reviewed great Mountain verse we saw how Jesus chastised his listeners by reminding them: "I have spoken to you of earthly things and you do not believe; how then will you believe if I speak of heavenly things?" And we now find Him making a very bold and tangible promise very early in the *New Testament* that "all these things will be given" to those diligently seeking the kingdom of God and His righteousness.

"Well, I can't see how this is even possible" many professing Christians will say (including, sadly, many preachers!). "It is easy to believe Jesus can and will save us when we die, but believe He will give us everything now? I work hard for what I have! It is unbelievable that we should expect Jesus to give us everything we need!" Yes, it is unbelievable as we are so often wrongly taught what *we must do* for God, not what He, here and now, does for us.

This is the attitude we should expect when we do not know, are not told and taught:

- ✓ Jesus' warning, "You have a fine way of rejecting the commandment of God in order to establish your own traditions!"

83

✓ The 1st recorded public Word of Jesus "Repent," meaning most notably, that we are totally helpless and hopeless **both now and eternally** without Him.

✓ "The law was given through Moses; grace and truth came through Jesus Christ"

✓ What Grace is.

✓ To Whom God gives Grace.

✓ Where, in *God's Word*, is His best "picture" of salvation and that this salvation begins when we are born again and only culminates when we die and are eternally glorified (or more rightly said, ends for "earthly things" when we die and becomes even greater Grace when we are then glorified).

✓ We are Saved and live BY grace.

✓ We are saved FOR: "to do the good works God planned in advance for us to do." To have both the time and necessary resources we must, then necessarily, be <u>given</u> all we need to both physically survive and do these good works.

✓ "The work of God is to believe in the one he sent," His Son and His promises (including providing everything we now require) – this believing is the highest and ultimate work we are assigned to do.

✓ "The word of God is living and active" and absolutely required as a guide in our servant life.

✓ "And now, Israel [today – Christian] what does the Lord your God ask of you but to fear the Lord your God, to walk in obedience to him, to love him, to serve the Lord your God with all your heart and with all your soul, and to observe the Lord's commands and decrees that I am giving you today **for your own good**?" and

✓ That when we hear His Voice we must not harden our hearts, but must "Repent" again and again and again – that "If you love me, you will keep my commandments," including for our "earthly things" because, if we do not believe these "how then will you believe if I speak of heavenly things?"

These verses form an unbroken and complementary "Mountain range" of great theme truths that help us see lesser related truths, but are also necessary to begin to see God's full Gospel message.

Now to a well-known but, in a sense, very unfamiliar and untaught to any meaningful depth, great Mountain verse . . .

18. "In the beginning God _____."

"Of course, I know this fill-in-the-blank! Do you think I am a dunce?" Everybody seemingly knows this opening verse of *God's Word*. But far fewer are taught its great significance and necessity for an authentic working faith. And most people, Christian and non-Christian, have an opinion [not real faith or good reason] based on little thought – they simply casually and superficially either accept or reject it. This is a clear case of some saying we know and believe a claim without really considering its significance and real, thought-through, impact. It is kind of like the feeling is: "So what? What difference does it *really* make to believe or not believe this?"

For while most professing Christians (some do not) "know and believe" *Genesis 1:1* we can *really*, at most, only understand a very small part of it. But to the extent we can understand it, it is important we do since **our faith cannot exceed our belief in God's sovereignty and the greatest demonstration of God's sovereignty is His creation of the heavens and earth** (and His promise to create a new heaven and earth at the end of time). *Genesis 1:1* highlights what "faith" and "believing" mean; believing *beyond* what we can fully understand in contrast to an all-too-common false faith being that which we can (or think we can) understand, grasp and explain.

> By faith we understand that the universe was formed at God's command, so that what is seen was not made out of what was visible. Heb 11:3

"My thoughts are not your thoughts,
    neither are your ways My ways,"
     declares the LORD.
"For as the heavens are higher than the earth,
    so My ways are higher than your ways,
    and My thoughts than your thoughts." Is 55:8-9

God's Word does not tell us how, but it certainly does tell us many times that God can "connect" with *everyone* more closely than we can relate to any other single person. And unlike us, who often find it hard to concentrate on a single other person (or even on ourself!) with life's many distractions, God's awareness and concentration on *every* person at all times is not hard for Him, it is just Who He is, it is *natural* for Him. Thus, He can love, converse in prayer, guide, lead, control . . . *everyone* at the same time with no effort on His part. And His sovereignty is not just related to individual people, but includes all animals, flowers . . . Everything that exists is within God's consciousness at all times. "Every shell has a story" Unknown and all these stories are ultimately written by God. And while we, as humans, can turn our backs to God we cannot "walk away from" Him since He is sovereign over everything and everyone at all times.

A second proof of this all-the-time connection with everyone is that it must be true if God is sovereign over everything because anyone is *only* truly sovereign to the extent they are minutely aware of and control something (in the case of God everything at all times). Is God's very real sovereignty over everyone and everything unfathomable? Of course. Which is why faith (Grace-faith, that which is given by God) is the only means of accepting this and the many verses in *God's Word* based on this truth. And as we live the Christian life, experience will confirm this great truth – God is watching and protecting us at all times, a very comforting thought for believers!

While the Earth is Small the Universe is VERY VERY Big

There are many credible estimates of the number of galaxies and stars. One such estimate is that of David Kornreich (founder of the Ask an Astronomer program at Cornell University). He estimates there are 10 trillion galaxies in the universe. Multiplying that by the Milky Way's (our galaxy) estimated 100 billion stars results in a very very large number: 1,000,000,000,000,000,000,000,000 possible stars. And Prof. Kornreich feels the number is likely even higher with more recent studies showing ever-increasing numbers of galaxies.

So, if God can make in excess of 1,000,000,000,000,000,000,000,000 stars (an estimated 9.3 trillion stars for every one of the projected 107 billion people who have ever lived – or putting this in a context we might better comprehend, almost 3,900 stars for every second of the 107 billion people who have lived) and all the while He is controlling them (stars and people) how can we doubt (even if we cannot comprehend) He can do anything, that He is truly sovereign?

This helps make sense of the following teaching of Jesus that just as nothing is too big for God, nothing is too small – He is sovereign over all:

"Are not two sparrows sold for a penny? Yet not one of them will fall to the ground apart from the will of your Father. And even the very hairs of your head are all numbered. So don't be afraid; you are worth more than many sparrows." Mt 10:29-31

And at the other end of the size spectrum, we can see that the micro (DNA) is maybe even more marvelous, intricate, well-designed and unbelievable than the universe with its incomprehensible number of stars. For we are told the average human body has 37 trillion cells containing a combined 10 to 20 billion miles of DNA (God's personal and unique paint brush for each person) within these cells.

No, we cannot comprehend even a small part of this (large or small) reality, but we can and should seek to find and practice the clear "earthly," and therefore testable, promises of Christ based on the realities of a God with these sovereign powers – this is our Grace-faith. And as we see His "earthly things" promises consistently coming true this should spur us on to an even greater interest and urgency in pursuing Him. This is how faith grows step-by-step to the point we realize there is much about God, Christ and the Holy Spirit we can't understand or comprehend, but we can see and experience the supernatural and personal love and presence of God in our lives and hunger and thirst for more of Him.

One practical way to increase our faith in *Genesis 1:1* is to contemplate its antithesis and its far greater unbelievability: that nothing was "sitting" around one day and without any outside influence this nothing all of a sudden exploded into both all we now see and that which is so small it is beyond our seeing! Believing "In the beginning, God created . . ." is **far more** credible, especially as we learn and find His Word increasingly and personally true in our lives.

Interestingly, however, it is often easier to believe God can do the big and macro (creating the heaven and earth) while doubting He is interested in and can handle the seemingly unlimited small details in the lives of literally billions of living people. And counterintuitively, it is often easier to "believe" in these great "cosmic" truths versus having faith in God's promised "earthly things" provisions we looked at earlier. Or believing for others while having doubts and being confused in the middle of our own trials.

Saving faith, a living sovereign God-given Grace-faith, grows by experience in seeing His impossible, miraculous, inexplicable promises being fulfilled time and again. And as this happens, we develop a faith in what we cannot comprehend as a basis for personal faith in our lives and problems – we develop faith to test God's *Word* promises that the unbeliever scoffs at as impossible and therefore foolish. And in one respect they are right while in another:

> "With man this is impossible [the salvation of our souls as well as the multitude of God's other promises], but with God all things are possible." Mt 19:26

And not even our saving Grace-faith is possible, rather:

> ". . . this is not from yourselves, it is the gift of God." Eph 2:8

Contemplating the great truth that "In the beginning God created the heavens and the earth" is a practical way to remind ourselves God is sovereign infinitely more than all men who have ever lived combined – He is likewise infinitely more powerful than Satan and his herd of fallen angels. This is the practical reality of the One we look to for Provision, Protection and Purpose.

"In the beginning God created the heavens and the earth" is a great Mountain verse most often either superficially "believed" or simply ignored instead of frequently contemplated in building a working faith. It is obviously considered great and important by God since He chose to make this the very first truth claim of His Word, an assertion non-believers consider impossible and a fable. And if they are correct, that God's first words are a lie, any further claims we find in *God's Word* are meaningless. On the other hand, if a professing Christian claims to believe it, any doubt about the miracles of Jesus is foolish because they are mere child's play in comparison to His creating the heavens and earth!

19. Jesus says: "_____ whoever blasphemes against
the Holy Spirit will never be forgiven; he is guilty of an eternal sin."

Maybe the Most Encouraging Verses in *God's Word*

We have looked at a number of great Mountain verses that for whatever reason we are not taught (or explained to anywhere near their fullest meaning) while contemplating other Mountain verses often considered as molehills because we are not taught their punchlines, the last portion that makes them so powerful and important. For example, in the first case below, few people are told and taught the "for" of our salvation so we can run around mistakenly trying to figure what our purpose is or wrongly think maybe, by being born again, everything important is completed – WRONG! And in the second, widely-known, passage we have probably heard, read and largely grasped it with the exception of the last, icing on the cake, four words.

For we are God's handiwork, created in Christ Jesus to do good works, which God prepared in advance for us to do.

And now, Israel [today – Christian] what does the Lord your God ask of you but to fear the Lord your God, to walk in obedience to him, to love him, to serve the Lord your God with all your heart and with all your soul, and to observe the Lord's commands and decrees that I am giving you today **for your own good**?

In the case we are looking at here, we have all been told (if in church any length of time) of the unforgivable sin, blasphemy of the Holy Spirit. As a result, we know (even if not the exact words) "whoever blasphemes against the Holy Spirit will never be forgiven; he is guilty of an eternal sin." But we seldom hear a clear explanation of what this unforgivable sin is. Nor do we hear the preface of this passage, which makes this otherwise "downer" passage possibly the most encouraging verse in *God's Word:*

> "**All the sins and blasphemies of men will be forgiven them**. But whoever blasphemes against the Holy Spirit will never be forgiven; he is guilty of an eternal sin." Mk 3:28-29

This same exact great blessing said in a more familiar way?

> "Therefore, **there is now <u>no condemnation for those who are in Christ Jesus</u>**, because through Christ Jesus the law of the Spirit of life set me free from the law of sin and death." Ro 8:1-2

"No condemnation" – "all sins will be forgiven" . . . "for those who are in Christ Jesus." Taken together these promises tell us that "**there is now** no condemnation for those who are in Christ Jesus," with this promise extending through all of eternity.

"WOW," did Jesus say and mean that? "All the sins and blasphemies of men will be forgiven them." HOW/WHY then, we have to ask ourselves, do we hear so much about certain specific sins when Jesus is clearly saying here that <u>all sins will be forgiven with only blasphemy against the Holy Spirit being the **single** eternally deadly sin</u>? Aren't "all sins" essentially molehills in comparison to blasphemy against the Holy Spirit? For even blasphemy of the Father and Jesus will be forgiven as well as:

- Making and worshipping idols,
- Improperly using God's name,
- Dishonoring father and mother,
- Murder,
- Adultery (and all other sexual sins, however gross),
- Stealing,
- Lying,
- Coveting,
- ALL sins.

So, What Exactly is Blasphemy of the Holy Spirit?

And it should be obvious why this is the only unforgivable sin. "**All the sins and blasphemies of men will be forgiven them,**" for those humbling themselves (God gives Grace to the humble), repenting, accepting Jesus' sacrifice on the cross as payment for their sins (great and small – past, current and future), versus those who, in pride, reject this offer of God's Holy Spirit, the Giver of spiritual life and as a result remain unforgiven and forever guilty.

One serious current and common blasphemy (rejection) of the Holy Spirit is teaching that we can "accept" Jesus as our Savior and enjoy all the benefits of eternal salvation without His being our LORD – it is blasphemy in both the teaching and attempted living of this error. There are clear necessities and signs of authentic saving (Grace-given) faith: living by, in and through the Holy Spirit being the key sign.

We are saved by a Grace – God gives grace to the humble. Blasphemy of the Holy Spirit is the flip side of God gives Grace to the humble – He does not give Grace to those who, in pride, blaspheme the Holy Spirit (reject Him because they see no need of Him) for the Holy Spirit is the *only* One Who applies Jesus' offered grace and truth to every Christian – if we are saved we are indwelled by the Holy Spirit/if we are not indwelled by the Holy Spirit we are not saved.

> Now it is God who establishes both us and you in Christ. He anointed us, placed His seal on us, and put His Spirit in our hearts as **a pledge** of what is to come. 2Cor 1:21-22

> You also were included in Christ when you heard the message of truth, the gospel of your salvation. When you believed, you were marked in him with a seal, the promised Holy Spirit, who is **a deposit guaranteeing our inheritance** until the redemption of those who are God's possession – to the praise of his glory. Ephesians 1:13-14

In a very real sense, we can say, our connection to God the Father and Jesus Christ is via the

Holy Spirit – for only through the Holy Spirit will we hear, understand and find God's Grace-faith and power to do what God tells us in His Word.

Psalm 23 is a good portrait of the Holy Spirit – He is the One who shepherds (provides for and protects us), "makes us . . . leads us . . . restores us . . . guides us . . . comforts us . . . anoints us . . ." and ultimately walks ahead, beside and behind us so we safely reach and enter the gates of heaven.

> The LORD is my shepherd, I shall not be in want.
> He makes me lie down in green pastures,
> he leads me beside quiet waters,
> he restores my soul.
> He guides me in paths of righteousness
> for his name's sake.
> Even though I walk
> through the valley of the shadow of death,
> I will fear no evil,
> for you are with me; your rod and your staff, they comfort me.
> You prepare a table before me
> in the presence of my enemies.
> You anoint my head with oil;
> my cup overflows.

> Surely goodness and love will follow me
>> all the days of my life,
> and I will dwell in the house of the LORD forever."

The Holy Spirit is likewise the sole source of the fruit of the Spirit that increases as we grow in God's Grace and knowledge of Christ [2Pe 3:18] – God's:

> "Love, joy, peace, patience, kindness, goodness, faithfulness, gentleness and self-control. Against such things there is no law. Those who belong to Christ Jesus have crucified the sinful nature with its passions and desires. <u>Since we live by the Spirit</u>, let us keep in step with the Spirit." [Gal 5:22-25]

Not accepting God's Holy Spirit leaves us in the unsaved state of:

> The acts of the flesh are obvious: sexual immorality, impurity and debauchery; idolatry and witchcraft; hatred, discord, jealousy, fits of rage, selfish ambition, dissensions, factions and envy; drunkenness, orgies, and the like. I warn you, as I did before, that **those who live like this will not inherit the kingdom of God.** [Gal 5:19-21]

Forever Lost, Apart from Christ.

While, from time to time, this very fearful warning of the blasphemy of the Holy Spirit is mentioned in church, very very seldom is this sin clearly explained, and it isn't explained precisely because the first half of the passage is overlooked as a molehill, not the high Mountain truth it is on which the second half of the passage hangs. And this first half of the passage is probably the most encouraging verse in *God's Word* and very important to keep us from running down many dead-end rabbit trails trying to please God by, in ourselves – without the Holy Spirit, thinking we can conquer our sins.

Thus, our focus and emphasis should be on the cause and cure of sin – true salvation (being truly born again) assures the promised indwelling Holy Spirit and His life-long leading to a growing in the grace and knowledge of Christ [2Pe 3:18] – this is the anti-blasphemy of the Holy Spirit and only "ticket" to eternal salvation.

You, however, are controlled not by the sinful nature but by the Spirit, if the Spirit of God lives in you. And **if anyone does not have the Spirit of Christ, he does not belong to Christ**. [Ro 8:9]

Those who are led by the Spirit of God are sons of God. [Ro 8:14]

No one knows the thoughts of God except the Spirit of God. We have not received the spirit of the world but the Spirit who is from God, that we may understand what God has freely given us. This is what we speak, not in words taught us by human wisdom but in words taught by the Spirit, expressing spiritual truths in spiritual words. The man without the Spirit does not accept the things that come from the Spirit of God, for they are foolishness to him, and he cannot understand them, because they are spiritually discerned. [1Co 2:11-14]

To each one the manifestation of the Spirit is given for the common good. To one there is given through the Spirit the message of wisdom, to another the message of knowledge by means of the same Spirit, to another faith by the same Spirit, to another gifts of healing by that one Spirit, to another miraculous powers, to another prophecy, to another distinguishing between spirits, to another speaking in different kinds of tongues, and to still another the interpretation of tongues. All these are the work of one and the same Spirit, and he gives them to each one, just as he determines. 1Co 12:7-11

In "talking" to ourselves and others, therefore, we must keep this full great Mountain passage in mind – "**All the sins and blasphemies of men will be forgiven them**. But whoever blasphemes against the Holy Spirit will never be forgiven; he is guilty of an eternal sin." Because, to the extent the devil can keep us focused on our sins (as he most often does for the religious) we are no better off than the unsaved who deny their sin or feel their good works make up for their "slip ups." Therefore, when being confronted with the world's inevitable and many "What do you think about X [typically the current hot button issues]" our focus should be Jesus' emphasis: "**All the sins and blasphemies of men will be forgiven them**. But whoever blasphemes against the Holy Spirit will never be forgiven; he is guilty of an eternal sin."

If, in contrast, we mistakenly foundationally think, teach or preach against any particular sin(s) it will be a weak to false "gospel" for there are literally thousands of different sins. Our focus must be on seeking to live in, by and through God's Holy Spirit as our only hope of eternal salvation. Power in the authentic Christian life comes solely by and through the indwelling Holy

Spirit.

The kingdom of God is not a matter of talk but of <u>power</u>. 1 Cor 4:20

In the last days terrible times will come. For men will be lovers of themselves, lovers of money, boastful, arrogant, abusive, disobedient to their parents, ungrateful, unholy, unloving, unforgiving, slanderous, without self-control, brutal, without love of good, traitorous, reckless, conceited, lovers of pleasure rather than lovers of God, <u>having a form of godliness but denying its power</u>. Turn away from such as these! 2 Tim 3:1-5

I ask that out of the riches of His glory He may strengthen you with <u>power through His Spirit</u> . . . that you may be filled with all the fullness of God . . . according to His <u>power</u> that is at work within us. Eph 3:16-20

So, to repeat: there is no higher or more important and encouraging passage in *God's Word* than:

"All the sins and blasphemies of men will be forgiven them. But whoever blasphemes against the Holy Spirit will never be forgiven; he is guilty of an eternal sin."

Thus, the goal of our faith, the salvation of our souls, is predicated on our accepting and living by God's Holy Spirit as opposed to blaspheming the Holy Spirit which is the case when we think we can "go it alone" without His life-giving presence in and with us.

100

Like the proverbial broken record: it is frustrating, perplexing, bewildering, disappointing, exasperating, shocking and very frightening (all of these and more) that this great Mountain truth is not fully and regularly taught to make sure we do not fail in this singularly important matter, the only sin God does not forgive!

The following is a link to a very good sermon entitled *How to Seek the Holy Spirit* if you have a few minutes to watch it:

https://youtu.be/xqgeT26BAnE

20. *The Great Juxtaposed Mountains*

Apart from me you _____. I can do everything through _____.

When confronted with the Mountain verses and passages we have been looking at they will certainly surprise those who have not read *God's Word* – for these are indeed very big, bold and precise truths, unlike the caricature of theoretical, ethereal, out-of-date religious rules so often expected. And for those who have read *God's Word* and listened to many sermons it will likewise be surprising, once highlighted, as to how and why these Mountain truths have been so routinely overlooked or treated as molehills.

We will now briefly look at a pair of verses that have also been largely ignored with the only reasonable explanation being that readers of *God's Word*, when they read them, don't *really* believe what is being said. For it they did, they could not restrain their excitement just as preachers, if they really believed them, would preach them often and boldly. And these two verses are even much grander when viewed side-by-side:

Apart from me [Jesus speaking] you can do **nothing**. Jn 15:5

I can do **everything** through him [Christ through His Holy Spirit] who gives me strength. Phil 4:13

If we cannot relate to these verses we have missed the core Christian message, the goal of the

Christian faith, the salvation of our souls and the promised gift of the Holy Spirit to accomplish this goal. In a sense, these great verses are simply practical consequences of **not** blaspheming the Holy Spirit.

It should not be so hard to believe if we are hearing from and experiencing God, Who created the heavens and earth, that:

> Apart from me you can do **nothing**. Jn 15:5

For Jesus has already warned of this early in *Matthew*:

> "Not everyone who says to me, 'Lord, Lord,' will enter the kingdom of heaven, **but only he who does the will of my Father who is in heaven**. Many will say to me on that day, 'Lord, Lord, did we not prophesy in your name, and in your name drive out demons and perform many miracles?' Then I will tell them plainly, 'I never knew you. Away from me, you evildoers!'" Mt 7:21-23

It is not, then, a matter of the quantity and size of the good works we do for God that "counts," but what is important is our faithfulness in completing the good works He specifically, precisely and personally prepared in advance for us to do in/by/through His Holy Spirit.

> I can do **everything** through him who gives me strength. Phil 4:13

The One through Whom we do anything meaningful is God's indwelling Holy Spirit:

> Unless the LORD builds the house,
>   the builders labor in vain. ^{Ps 127:1}

Haven't we been promised, in a number of Mountain verses we have looked at (as a theme of many other supporting verses in *God's Word*), that as servants of God He necessarily provides everything we need (most importantly the power, through His indwelling Holy Spirit) for doing the impossible. Every Christian is called frequently to do what is impossible for them to do without God's aiding Holy Spirit!

As servants of Christ, doing the good works God planned for us to do through His omnipotent Holy Spirit indwelling us, mustn't we believe these twin truths to be our realities? God expects this and so should we! Please preachers: highlight and teach us these great truths!

21. *"Resist the Devil, and He Will Flee from You."*

Do you really (can you reasonably) believe this? Are you experiencing this reality?

Before we wrap-up this very short overview of key *God's Word* Mountain verses (with three remaining examples), let's look at another important verse that also provides a lesson on how/why Mountain verses can instead seem and be treated as molehills.

Unlike many of the other Mountain verses we have looked at that are **not** well-known, "Resist the devil, and he will flee from you" is familiar to most professing Christians. But relatively few people seemingly know *how* to make this promise a consistent experience, thus they cannot believe it and, as such, it is more often a discouragement and doubt rather than encouragement, faith and reality.

Just as we tend to minimize the need of Christ and His Holy Spirit, we can likewise narrowly consider resisting the devil as an infrequent action when bad things happen to us. In practice and reality, however, if we are not NOW resisting the devil we will fall (or already have fallen) prey to him.

> "Sin is crouching at your door; it desires to have you, but you must master it." ^{Ge 4:7}

For **any time** we are not "in Christ" we are out of Christ. When we are not living by the Holy Spirit we are living apart from Him.

Likewise, the devil encourages "one-handed" faith because he knows it isn't effective. We are warned about this false notion:

- Faith by itself, if it does not have <u>works,</u> is dead. ^{Jas 2:17}
- "Not everyone who says to Me, 'Lord, Lord,' will enter the kingdom of heaven, **but only he who does the will of My Father in heaven** [the good works He planned in advance specifically and personally planned for every Christian – not what they decide are the good works they will do]. Many will say to Me on that day, 'Lord, Lord, did we not prophesy in Your name, and in Your name drive out demons and perform many miracles?'
Then I will tell them plainly, 'I never knew you; depart from Me, you workers of lawlessness!" ^{Mt 7:21-23}

Another common deadly falsehood the devil misleads by (as we have looked at earlier) is the common "belief" that "spiritual" issues are simply mental, largely theoretical and ethereal (heavenly) while "power" and "earthly things" sound too "practical" and not very Christianly to many professing people.

So, the "when" of resisting the devil is: always. The "how" is what sadly is also seldom told and taught, making "Resist the devil, and he will flee from you" a mere molehill if not "sandwiched" between its two how-to conditions:

[1.] **Submit yourselves, then, to God.**

Resist the devil, and he will flee from you.

[2.] **Draw near to God, and He will draw near to you.** ^{Ja 4:7-8}

And these make obvious **why** the devil will flee: he is not fleeing from us, rather the devil is only going to flee from anyone submitted to and thus near God – he has no fear of us, but he is dreadfully fearful of being near God (like the 6th grade bully not being fearful of the 90-pound weakling classmate, but who dares not try anything when the weaker child's father or big brother is present).

Having the devil flee from us is a Grace of God and all Graces are freely offered, yet all-the-same they require we value, take and protect them through continuing and related Graces; they have conditions attached to them. This, again, explains why we must be "in *God's Word*," so when we are in need of one of His Grace-promises we know the conditions accompanying them, the keys to "unlocking" them. It is important we know the great promises of God, but to make them the Mountains they can be we **must** know the surrounding conditions as well. It is like being given a car by our parents with a credit card in the glove compartment, ALL grace. We are not going too far or too long unless we periodically stop, use the credit card (provided by the parents) to fill the gas tank – likewise, we are not going to go far or long spiritually if we are not in Christ.

"**Submit yourselves, then, to God**. Resist the devil, and he will flee from you. **Draw near to God, and He will draw near to you**" is yet another important 24/7/365 passage we need to be taught in its fullness and reminded of frequently. And since there are many such verses in *God's Word*, the only way we can expect to be regularly reminded of them is to be reading *God's*

Word personally and consistently! While we have a legitimate complaint that churches should be teaching and preaching the Mountain verses more, no one has a valid criticism if they are not equally taking responsibility for their salvation by reading *God's Word* on a regular basis. For, if we were, we would also find (with the help of the Holy Spirit) our next great, seldom preached and taught, Mountain verse.

22. There remains, then, a _____ for the people of God.

The *4th Commandment*:

> Remember the Sabbath day by keeping it holy. Six days you shall labor and do all your work, but the seventh day is a Sabbath to the LORD your God. On it you shall not do any work, neither you, nor your son or daughter, nor your manservant or maidservant, nor your animals, nor the alien within your gates. For in six days the LORD made the heavens and the earth, the sea, and all that is in them, but he rested on the seventh day. Therefore the LORD blessed the Sabbath day and made it holy." Ex 20:8-11 & Du 5:12-15

Interestingly, of the *Ten Commandments*, the 4th is the one most considered as no longer valid and observable. And this is interesting since the blessing of the Sabbath is thought of as a curse by so many people, even people who regularly attend church – as if "working like the devil" seven days a week is to be prized and emulated. Go figure.

It is noteworthy, then, that we find the following verse in the *New Testament*:

> There remains, then, a Sabbath-rest for the people of God; for anyone who enters God's rest also rests from their works, just as God did from his. Heb 4:9-10

So, what do we do with this verse and the great chapter in which we find it? The very general approach? Radio silence! "Let's not draw attention to it since we don't believe in the blessing of God's Sabbath Commandment. Shhh!"

Instead, if considered rightly, we would see this is yet another example in which the *New Testament* "ups" the teachings of the *Old Testament* (not weaken or negate them!) based on Jesus' greater offered Grace. It is as if, in this verse, God is saying (as Jesus repeatedly says in His *Sermon on the Mount*): "You have heard it said . . . but I tell you [a far 'harder' command and blessing made possible by His Grace] . . ." In the Spirit of the New Covenant: Entering into God's Sabbath-rest is a "step up" from the Old Covenant. Christians are now offered (and the Master expects them to live in) a 24/7/365 Sabbath-rest ~ in a sense we are always to be in God's rest. **God is not stressing Monday – Saturday (much less Sunday) and neither should we be!**

We are not told and taught the great Mountain verses that make this impossibility a reality and necessity of authentic Christians because:

- ✓ We have failed to heed Jesus' great warning, "You have a fine way of rejecting the commandment of God in order to establish your traditions!"

- ✓ A common example being ignoring Jesus' 1st recorded public Word, "Repent," and the on-going necessity that it is.
- ✓ While routinely rejecting that which Jesus came to offer: "The law was given through Moses; grace and truth came through Jesus Christ."
- ✓ Few are told and taught what we are saved FOR: "to do the good works God planned in advance for us to do." And that to have both the time and required resources God must certainly give us **all** we need to live on and to do these good works.
- ✓ That "the work of God is to believe in the one he sent," His Son – this is the highest, ultimate and on-going work we are assigned to do. Every good work we do if for this ultimate purpose.
- ✓ "The word of God is living and active" and absolutely required as a guide in our servant life. That every "jot and tittle" of *God's Word* is given "for your own good." And that when we hear His Voice we must not harden our hearts – that "If you love me, you will keep my commandments," including the many "earthly things" promises and commands, for if we do not believe these "how then will you believe if I speak of heavenly things?"
- ✓ God is sovereign, working through us, giving us everything we need to do all He asks of, and prepared in advance for, us to do.

111

This allows us to rest 24/7/365 in a God-centered and focused Sabbath-rest. For, only in trusting in God, in His indwelling Holy Spirit and His power, can we rest while, at the same time, accomplish all God intends for us – the paradox of Grace.

The common theme? We so commonly ignore or twist many of God's very great and precise Mountain verses as being impossible and thus "too good to be true" which would be the case **except** they are real and testable as we will find precisely the point of our next to last Mountain verse.

23. *"Whoever Lives by the Truth Comes into the Light, so that _____."*

The Christian faith would be a shell of itself (much like all other religions) without the great Mountain promises and truths we have very briefly been reviewing. And it is a shell and façade even for those claiming themselves "Christian" not knowing, not caring they do not know and not practicing these great imperatives of the faith.

In one of the great Mountain-range chapters of *God's Word* (*John 3*), Jesus promises:

> "Whoever lives by the truth comes into the light, so that **it may be seen plainly that what he has done has been done through God**." Jn 3:21

mirrored by the complementary truth that:

> The kingdom of God is not a matter of talk but of **power**. 1 Cor 4:20

And exactly why are these great truths so routinely ignored and not taught? Because they are only of value when Grace-faith is real and active (and it is not real without being active). The "faith" of all other (false) religions must, therefore, be a matter of talk so that a caricature of Christianity, based on mere talk, is often accepted as valid when it clearly is not. False religions (including a phony "Christianity") make great promises for when we die and supposedly go to heaven, but none challenge us as Jesus does because they are not supported by any earthly reality or God-supporting Grace and power:

"I have spoken to you of earthly things and you do not believe; how then will you believe if I speak of heavenly things?" Jn 3:12

"Everyone who <u>hears these words of mine</u> **and** <u>puts them into practice</u> is like a wise man who built his house on the rock. The rain came down, the streams rose, and the winds blew and beat against that house; yet it did not fall, because it had its foundation on the rock." Mt 7:24-25

False religions simply cannot make similar claims because they will, if tried, show themselves powerless and empty.

Others may, if they know us closely and intimately, see miraculous changes that only authentic faith in THE true God can accomplish while most others, less intimately and closely connected to us, will likely not these changes. But **we** will certainly see great changes resulting as we repeatedly and continually "Repent" as led by the Holy Spirit in His sanctification of us. We do not have to depend on wondering if what we read in *God's Word* is true, He provides tangible evidence as we see God doing in and through us that which is impossible for us without Him! True Christian faith is neither a leap into darkness nor walking in darkness, it is coming "into the light," brighter and clearer, as we hear **His Voice**, learn, are led and live by **His Grace, Truth and Word** more and more.

It is frustrating that we are not taught this great truth early, soon after we are born again, to be on the lookout for the evidence that will "be seen **plainly** that what [we have] done has been done through God." This will confirm we are on the road of accomplishing the goal of our faith, the salvation of our souls – it is our basis for periodically examining and testing ourselves as we are told in the last Mountain verse, in the next chapter, in our short overview of God's Mountain verses.

24. "Examine yourselves to see _____."

A key teaching in many churches today is the importance of having an assurance of our salvation, and this is important for confidence and motivation to continue our Christian "walk:"

> Let us draw near to God with a sincere heart and with the <u>full assurance</u> that faith brings, having our hearts sprinkled to cleanse us from a guilty conscience and having our bodies washed with pure water. Heb 10:22

The result, however, is that untold numbers of people with no basis, in *God's Word,* for an assurance of faith and salvation are nonetheless satisfied and confident they are "saved." A truthless assurance is a dangerous and, unless corrected, ultimately an eternally deadly belief. The Biblical model for making sure our faith is authentic is that we periodically examine ourselves with an assurance resulting from an objective (outside our feelings or others' nice comments) analysis:

> **Examine <u>yourselves</u>** to see whether you are in the faith; **<u>test yourselves</u>**. Do you not realize that Christ Jesus is in you – unless, of course, you fail the test? 2Cor 13:5

Test ourselves? How? There are so many voices and opinions about what is right, who should we believe? **Where can we look to examine ourselves to see if our faith is valid or false? By and through *God's Word* of course.**

Most people try, at some point, to read *God's Word*, only to get confused or bored, not seeing anything really meaningful or overly helpful in it – they often hear in church (of course, picking and choosing and rejecting the ideas that don't seem right for one reason or another) political, philosophical, psychological, just opinions . . ..

A valid examination, however, must include asking ourselves if we are living the great Mountain truths of *God's Word*. Do these great Mountain truths resonate, enlighten and encourage us? Do they make us want to know more and experience them to a greater degree? Are they increasingly (in sanctification) becoming more of us? Every one of these verses (and many others we will encounter in regular reading of *God's Word*) are helpful in examining ourselves to make sure we are in the faith:

- ✓ Are we increasingly mastering, by Grace (through an indwelling and leading Holy Spirit), <u>the</u> sin (first and foremost blasphemy of the Holy Spirit manifesting itself in one of many possible ways) that is crouching at our personal door and desires "to have us?"

117

✓ Are we seeing and experiencing the fruit of, more and more, repentance to the commandments of God versus the natural tendency of rejecting God in favor of a number of religious traditions?

✓ Is our goal God's defined goal of our faith, "the salvation of our soul?"

✓ Are we better understanding the critical on-going necessity of repenting as Jesus tells us in His 1st recorded public Word command?

✓ Through practice are we increasingly learning and living Jesus' Grace and Truth? And as well, is this making us more and more humble as we increasingly see our impotence and God's offer of His power for and in us?

✓ In periodic and consistent reading of *God's Word*, are we testing ourselves against *God's Word's* best "picture" of salvation?

✓ Are we seeing how we have been, are and will be fully saved BY Grace?

✓ As we mature in God's Grace-faith, are we better aware of what we are saved FOR: "to do the good works God prepared in advance for us to do" – the very precise good works as personal as our unique fingerprints and DNA?

✓ Is our primary day-to-day work focused on believing "in the One He sent" – His Son?

✓ Among the many voices we hear, is it progressively clear "The word of God is living and active" – unique **and necessary** to living the Christian life?

✓ Have we finally reached the point that we understand all "the Lord's commands and decrees that I am [God] giving you today **are for our own good**," not penalties or sacrifices we supposedly make for God? And that this faith has not come by understanding all aspects of everything we face in life, but in knowing and loving God?

✓ Is our desire to better know what Jesus says in His Word because we understand "If you love me, you will you will keep my commandments?"

✓ That we are expected to "Today, if you hear his voice, do not harden your hearts," but to seek and welcome His always good and loving direction?

✓ That Jesus has primarily "spoken to you of earthly things," warning rhetorically: "and if you do not believe; how then will you believe if I speak of heavenly things?"

✓ That in this vein, do we now grasp the very vital offer necessary for fulfilling a successful Christian paradigm that we "seek first the kingdom of God and His righteousness" so that "all these things [ALL our earthly material needs and more] will be given to you as well?"

✓ As we look for and experience God's sovereignty on a regular basis, are we gaining a greater appreciation for "In the beginning God created the heavens and the earth" and the significance of this truth, and our believing it as a basis for faith that God can do everything, in, by and through us – nothing being impossible for Him, absolutely nothing! That based on this we now know that apart from Christ we can do nothing, while likewise understanding we can do everything through the Holy Spirit who gives us the required strength (and provisions) to do all the good works God planned in advance for us to do?

✓ That thinking otherwise, that we can "do life ourselves," is blasphemy of the Holy Spirit?

✓ Do we greatly fear blasphemy of the Holy Spirit while, at the same time, find Jesus' warning in this respect so encouraging because it means **all** other sins will be forgiven – so we can concentrate on and always be seeking the Holy Spirit?

✓ As we opened up above, are we increasingly mastering the sin that is crouching at our personal door and desires "to have us?" Do we understand our greatest adversary is the devil so that we are following God's instructions for making the devil flee from us by submitting ourselves to God and drawing closer to Him?

✓ Day-by-day, through greater experience, is faith becoming less ethereal and theoretical and more obvious and practical – the only way to even imagine getting through life successfully? In other words, can we confess it is "plainly seen that what has been done has been done through God?" Jn 3:21

In a single great truth proclaimed by John the Baptist (notably the one of whom Jesus declared as "among those born of women there has not risen anyone greater than John the Baptist"), the

Christian life is maybe best pictured, proclaimed and examined for authenticity as a continuing, until we die, knowing and seeking for ourselves a: "He must become greater; I must become less" [Jn 3:30] mentality producing a growing in "the grace and knowledge of our Lord and Savior Jesus Christ." [2Pe 3:18] All making the Apostle Paul's confession our confession:

> Not that I have already obtained all this, or have already been made perfect, but I press on to take hold of that for which Christ Jesus took hold of me. Brothers, I do not consider myself yet to have taken hold of it. But one thing I do: Forgetting what is behind and straining toward what is ahead, I press on toward the goal to win the prize of God's heavenly calling in Christ Jesus. [Phil 3:12-14]

Yes, an assurance of faith is required to live a life of faith and the resulting good works emanating from this faith.

> We always thank God for all of you and continually mention you in our prayers. We remember before our God and Father your work produced by faith, your labor prompted by love, and your endurance inspired by hope in our Lord Jesus Christ. [1Th 1:2-3]

Periodic self-examination against *God's Word* is the **only** reliable basis for a successful examination to ensure we are indeed in the faith of eternal life.

25. Summary – Is God's Word Enough?

It should be apparent by now that the theme of this short book has been the importance of *God's Word* in the authentic Christian life. But have we over-emphasized its importance? Or asked another way: Is *God's Word* enough? And the clear answer is: "No, *God's Word*, as important as it is, is not the all-in-all of Christian faith." We know this because Jesus warned the Jewish leaders (as found in *John Chapter 5):*

> You study the Scriptures diligently because you think that in them you have eternal life. These are the very Scriptures that testify about me, yet you refuse to come to me to have life.

Eternal life is only by Christ through His Grace-faith. But, as the great Model, no one depended on and lived more by *God's Word* than Jesus.

So, we can rightly say, *God's Word* is necessary as a foundation and framework for knowing Jesus' Grace and Truth on a path of achieving the goal of Christian faith, the salvation of our souls. For, as Jesus proclaimed even before the first great Mountain verse we looked at (before His first recorded public Word, "Repent!"), in refuting the devil He repeated an *Old Testament* teaching:

> "Man shall not live on bread alone, but on every word that comes from the mouth of God." [Mt 4:4]

Celebration of *God's Word,* as a necessary foundation and framework for Christian life, is the attitude of authentic Christians. Yet, at no time in history have there been as many sources for "Christian" exchange of ideas – videos, podcasts, YouTube, radio and television, other books (we have even added to this as the following page of other books from Beulah State attests). As such, there is a great temptation to go to other sources for an understanding of what God says to us in His Word. So consider, which makes better sense: "Today I will read *God's Word*" or "Today I think I will listen to a sermon on-line or read a Christian book rather than reading *God's Word.*" Thinking about it like this the answer should be a no-brainer! Just the idea we can read *God's Word* ought to astound us. For those who have the time (after completing a day's *God's Word* reading discipline), other sources may be helpful, but they are all "gravy" to the "meat and potatoes" of *God's Word*!

It would be great for everything to be perfect in our Christian "walk" (that we attend the perfect church with the perfect pastor/preacher, we are never distracted in life away from God, that our developed disciplines . . . are faultless) but life never is perfect. To filter distractions, as said before, we must be well-schooled in and by *God's Word* to properly fact-check what we hear outside it, even by well-meaning supposed experts in *God's Word.*

Have I been frustrated by being so slow in "getting" the Mountain verses we have looked? Yes. Is this frustration lifting somewhat? Yes, thankfully. Because, in the final analysis, it has finally dawned on me that we are all **personally** responsible (under the leading and guidance of God Himself) for the working out of our salvation:

> Therefore, my beloved, just as you have always obeyed, not only in my presence, but now even more in my absence, continue to work out your salvation with fear and trembling. For it is God who works in you to will and to act on behalf of His good purpose. Phil 2:12-13

When I look back it can still be disheartening when I again realize the lost time (and potential opportunities forfeited) because simple key foundational verses and passages were not highlighted and understood early on and in some logical manner. Yet, thankfully, over many years a picture has begun to emerge.

All we need to know is not contained in the great Mountain verses of *God's Word* we have reviewed in this short write up. Rather, we can grasp (and the reality is that the best we will know, this side of heaven, is at best) a beginning knowledge of their fullness which will allow us to make far greater sense of *God's Word* (versus being led into and living in error and "molehill-land" based on traditions of man contrary to *God's Word*).

In our reading we will find other great Mountain verses we have not addressed here, the most obvious being the *Ten Commandments* also minimized more and more in recent years, since we have here concentrated on very great and virtually ignored verses and passages. Likewise, there are occasions where God will use an otherwise small and seemingly mundane verse as a Mountain in our personal life to answer a question or address a specific issue we face or may have.

So, life really comes down to the question of whether we are **personally** guided and led by the loosely-gooey, ever shifting and confusing ideas of the world (termed social proof – taking our "cues" in life by observing others) or if we make a decision to learn and live by *God's Word*, developing a discipline of seeking Him for His 24/7/365 guidance.

Our greatest prayer to the Only True and Triune God:

Open my eyes that I may see wonderful things in your law. Ps 119:18

Go to 789GracePlace.com (*Standing on Mountains* tab) for a downloadable printable listing of the Mountain verses we have looked at for future reference.

Other Books from Beulah State University Press @ *789GracePlace.com*

Time to Live
Making the Most of Our Time to Make the Most of Our Lives

Pursuing and Achieving Life's Greatest Possible Goal
A Few Bible Verses that Will Change Our Lives as We Better Understand and Apply Them

What I Wish I Had Been Told and Taught Soon After I Was Born Again

The Gospel of Better

Understanding This Christian Thing in the Present Tense
The Only Ultimate Hope and Help for Today and Forever!

Learning to Recognize and Follow the Footprint of Grace
Finding Grace in This Grace-Starved Age

Ten Great Disciplines of Christian Disciples

Ten Great Themes of the Bible

Ten Great Covenants of Jesus

The Map and Signs to the Greatest of All Possible Treasures

Chautauqua Headline News

Letters from Beulah State University

Overcoming the Obstacles to Successful Retirement

Made in the USA
Columbia, SC
19 February 2024